Edexcel GCSE
Religious Studies

Unit 2A
Religion and Life
Christianity

Christine Paul

A PEARSON COMPANY

Published by Pearson Education Limited, a company incorporated in England and Wales, having its registered office at Edinburgh Gate, Harlow, Essex, CM20 2JE. Registered company number: 872828

www.heinemann.co.uk

Edexcel is a registered trade mark of Edexcel Limited

Text © Pearson Education Ltd 2009
First published 2009

13 12 11 10 09
10 9 8 7 6 5 4 3 2 1

British Library Cataloguing in Publication Data
A catalogue record for this book is available from the British Library.
ISBN 978 1 84690 420 2

Edited by Florence Production Ltd
Typeset by HL Studios, Long Hanborough, Oxford
Original illustrations © Pearson Education Ltd 2009
Illustrated by HL Studios, Long Hanborough, Oxford
Cover design by Pearson Education Ltd
Picture research by Zooid
Cover photo/illustration © Naraphotography/Alamy
Printed in Italy by Rotolito Lombarda

Acknowledgements
The author and publisher would like to thank the following individuals and organisations for permission to reproduce photographs:

AFP/Getty Images/Jay Directo, p. 96; AFP/Getty Images/Joseph Barrak, p. 51; AFP/Getty Images/Kazuhiro Nogi, p. 20; age fotostock/Photolibrary Group/Henryk T Kaiser, p. 10; akg-images, p. 18; Alamy/Peter Barritt, p. 3; Alamy/Paul Glendell, p. 18; Alamy/John Glover, p. 95; Alamy/David J. Green – lifestyle themes, p. 18; Alamy/Glenn Harper, p. 31; allaction.co.uk / PA Photos/Anwar Hussein, p. 57; Arcaid/Corbis UK Ltd./Joe Cornish, p. 29; Arco Images GmbH/Alamy, p. 13; Aspa Films/Suevia Films S.A./ Ronald Grant Archive, p. 6; BBC Photograph Library, pp. 23, 57; BBC/Tiger Aspect Productions, p. 103; Blend Images/Alamy, p. 14; The Bridgeman Art Library/Getty Images, p. 84; Christina Saj Fine Art, p. 21; Classic Image/ Alamy, p. 84; ClassicStock/Alamy, p. 84; Corbis UK Ltd./John Lund, p. 3; Corbis UK Ltd./Dale C. Spartas, p. 29; CountrySideCollection/Alamy/ Homer Sykes, p. 23; Das Fotoarchiv/Still Pictures/Achim Pohl, p. 97; David Hoffman Photo Library/Alamy, p. 89; Design Pics Inc./Alamy, p. 33; Digital Vision, p. 13; Efe/Corbis UK Ltd./Ulises Rodriguez, p. 40; Epa/Corbis UK Ltd./Daniel Hambury, p. 67; Epa/Corbis UK Ltd./Mohammed Jalil, p. 18; Fotex/Rex Features, p. 71; The Gallery Collection/Corbis UK Ltd., p. 30; Getty Images/Jean-Marc Giboux, p. 49; Getty Images/Tim Graham, p. 84; Getty Images/Alex Wong, pp. 90–91; Godong/Corbis UK Ltd./Phillipe Lissac, p. 86; Hulton-Deutsch Collection/Corbis UK Ltd., p. 84; imagebroker/

Alamy, pp. 80–81; iStockphoto, p. 100; ITV/Rex Features, pp. 67, 75, 102; Liaison/Getty Images/Malcolm Linton, p. 18; Linographic, pp. 4–5, 13; The London Art Archive/Alamy, p. 19; Look and Learn/Bridgeman Art Library, p. 57; Megan Patricia Carter Trust/Sygma/Corbis UK Ltd./Kevin Carter, p. 47; Nic Cleave Photography/Alamy, pp. 28–29, 29, 40; PA Archive/PA Photos/Stefan Rousseau, p. 64; PA Photos, p. 84; PA Photos/John Birdsall, p.101; PA Photos/Doug Peters, p. 64; Pearson Education/Jules Selmes, p. 68; Photodisc, p. 13; Photoshot/Carl De Souza, p. 94; Reuters/Corbis UK Ltd., p. 45; Reuters/Corbis UK Ltd./Luke Macgregor, p. 89; Reuters/Corbis UK Ltd./Ian Waldie, p. 84; Revolution Studios and Columbia/akg-images, p. 58; Rex Features/Paul Grover, p. 19; Rex Features/Alisdair Macdonald, p. 8; Ronald Grant Archive, pp. 23, 35; Shutterstock, p. 31; Shutterstock/Yuri Arcurs, p. 84; Shutterstock/Jaroslaw Grudzinsk, p. 99; Snap/Rex Features, p. 43; Universal/Everett/Rex Features, pp. 16–17; Universal Pictures/ Album/akg-images, p. 3; www.art4us.me.uk/Gary Wakeham, p. 30; Zefa/ Corbis UK Ltd./Markus Moellenberg, p. 57.

The author also wishes to thank David Paul, Daniel Metcalfe, Bethany Metcalfe, Jonathan Paul and Emma Watson for their support and patience. She would also like to thank her colleagues and students at Bishopsgarth School.

Permissions acknowledgements
Scriptures quoted from The Youth Bible, New Century Version, copyright © 1991 by Word Publishing, a division of Thomas Nelson, Inc. Used by permission.

ASSIST Sheffield, from http://www.assistsheffield.org.uk/index. php?option=com_content&task=view&id=1&Itemid=1, pp. 92–3; Adapted from 'Blears's £50 million investment in community cohesion' at http:// www.communities.gov.uk/news/corporate/500395, © Crown copyright 2007, pp. 82–3; The Catechism of the Roman Catholic Church © 2002 by Continuum International Book Publishing Ltd, pp. 41, 44, 60, 65, 66, 91, 97; HMSO 'Fairness and Freedom: The final report of the equalities review', Crown copyright 2007, p. 83.

Click use licence number C2008002327.

Websites
There are links to relevant websites in this book. In order to ensure that the links are up to date, that the links work, and that the sites are not inadvertently linked to sites that could be considered offensive, we have made the links available on the Heinemann website at www.heinemann.co.uk/hotlinks. When you access the site, the express code is 4202P.

Disclaimer
This material has been published on behalf of Edexcel and offers high-quality support for the delivery of Edexcel qualifications.

This does not mean that the material is essential to achieve any Edexcel qualification, nor does it mean that it is the only suitable material available to support any Edexcel qualification. Edexcel material will not be used verbatum in setting any Edexcel examination or assessment. Any resource lists produced by Edexcel shall include this and other appropriate resources.

Copies of official specifications for all Edexcel qualifications may be found on the Edexcel website: www.edexcel.com

Contents

Welcome to this Edexcel GCSE in Religious Studies Resource

These resources have been written to support fully Edexcel's new specification for GCSE Religious Studies. Each student book covers one unit of the specification which makes up a Short Course qualification. Any two units from separate modules of the specification make up a Full Course qualification. Written by experienced examiners and packed with exam tips and activities, these books include lots of engaging features to enthuse students and provide the range of support needed to make teaching and learning a success for all ability levels.

Features in this book

In each section you will find the following features:

- **an introductory spread** which introduces the topics and gives the Edexcel key terms and learning outcomes for the whole section

- **topic spreads** containing the following features:

  - **Learning outcomes** for the topic

  - edexcel ⁞ key terms

    Specification key terms – are emboldened and defined for easy reference

  - **Glossary**

    Here we define other complex terms to help with understanding

  - **Activities** and **For discussion** panels provide stimulating tasks for the classroom and homework

  - a topic **Summary** which captures the main learning points.

How to use this book

This book supports Module A Unit 2 Religion and Life based on the study of Christianity. The unit requires students to study the relationships between Christianity and life in the UK. The diversity between the different Christian groups allows students to explore the significance and impact of the beliefs, teachings, sources, practices and ways of life and forms of expressing meaning. The unit asks students to express their personal responses to the issue raised, adopting an enquiring, critical and reflective approach to the study of Christianity.

This book is split into the four sections of the specification.

A dedicated suite of revision resources for complete exam success. We've broken down the six stages of revision to ensure that you are prepared every step of the way.

How to get into the perfect 'zone' for your revision.

Tips and advice on how to plan your revision effectively.

Revision activities and exam-style practice at the end of every section plus additional exam practice at the end of the book.

Last-minute advice for just before the exam.

An overview of what you will have to do in the exam, plus a chance to see what a real exam paper will look like.

What do you do after your exam? This section contains information on how to get your results and answers to frequently asked questions on what to do next.

ResultsPlus

These features are based on how students have performed in past exams. They are combined with expert advice and guidance from examiners to show you how to achieve better results.

There are five different types of ResultsPlus features throughout this book:

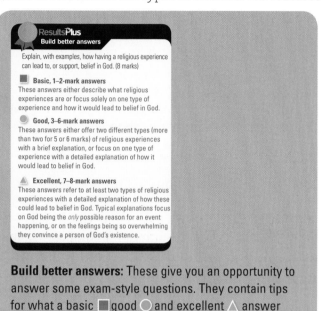

Build better answers: These give you an opportunity to answer some exam-style questions. They contain tips for what a basic ■ good ○ and excellent △ answer will contain.

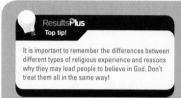

Top tip: These provide examiner advice and guidance to help improve your results.

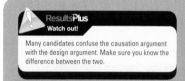

Watch out! These warn you about common mistakes and misconceptions that examiners frequently see students make. Make sure that you don't repeat them!

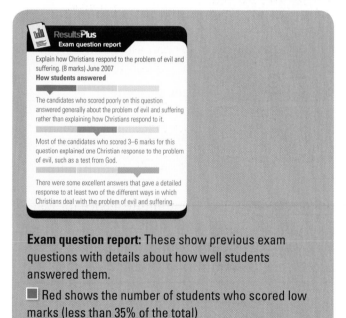

Exam question report: These show previous exam questions with details about how well students answered them.

■ Red shows the number of students who scored low marks (less than 35% of the total)

○ Orange shows the number of students who did okay (scoring between 35% and 70% of the total marks)

△ Green shows the number of students who did well (scoring over 70% of the total marks).

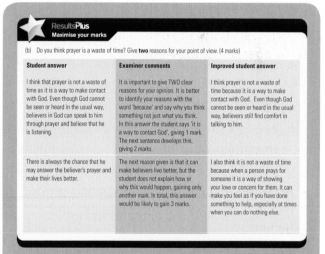

Maximise your marks: These are featured in the KnowZone at the end of each chapter. They include an exam-style question with a student answer, examiner comments and an improved answer so that you can see how to build a better response.

Believing in God

Introduction

In this section you will consider why some people do believe in God and why others do not. You will reflect on your own thoughts about God and what reasons and evidence you have for this viewpoint. You will learn about what Christians believe about God and the variety of reasons and evidence behind their beliefs. You will also learn about the things that challenge Christian beliefs about God and how Christians respond to these challenges.

Learning outcomes for this section

By the end of this section you will be able to:

- give definitions of the key terms and use them in answers to GCSE questions
- outline or describe the features of a Christian upbringing
- explain how people come to believe in God through having a Christian upbringing or a religious experience
- outline or describe different explanations of the origins of the universe, including the 'causation', 'design' and scientific arguments
- explain why scientific explanations of the origins of the universe cause some people to doubt God's existence, and how Christians respond to this
- outline or describe other examples of problems that may cause some people to doubt God's existence – for example, unanswered prayers, and evil and suffering
- explain how Christians respond to these arguments
- explain, with examples, how media programmes about religion may affect a person's attitude to belief in God
- express with reasons and evidence your own opinion about the reasons for believing or not believing in God, and your own thoughts about whether God exists or not.

edexcel ::: key terms

agnosticism	free will	natural evil	omnipotent
atheism	miracle	numinous	omniscient
conversion	moral evil	omni-benevolent	prayer

Each of these images represents what someone thinks God is like.

Fascinating fact

According to surveys in the UK, around 70 per cent of people claim to believe in some sort of God.

Which of the images on this page is the odd one out?

- Which is closest to your idea about God? Why?
- What questions do you think each image raises?

1.1 Christian upbringing and belief in God

Learning outcomes

By the end of this lesson, you should be able to:

- explain how your upbringing has contributed to making you the person you are today, giving examples of features of your own upbringing that have influenced you
- outline or describe the features of a Christian upbringing
- explain how a Christian upbringing may lead to or support belief in God
- give your opinion on religious upbringing.

Your upbringing

How you are brought up shapes the person you become. The way adults around you treat you, your experience of the world you encounter, things you are told and introduced to all contribute to the person you become. This is known as your 'culture'.

Activities

1 Think about your own childhood. Compare it to that of a young person growing up in America, Africa or India. What makes these young people different from you? You could do this by comparing the young people in the YouTube clip (www.heinemann.co.uk/hotlinks.express code 4202P).

2 Look at the poem below. Create your own poem identifying what makes you the person you are.

I am my older brother who first kicked a football at me...

I am my grandad who took me to my first football match...

I am my mother who loves me no matter what...

I am my father who is strong and secure...

I am my teacher who pushes me to be successful...

I am the Sunday School teacher who told me about God...

Glossary

Baptism – The Christian initiation ceremony that welcomes a person into the Christian community.

Confirmation – The service (sacrament) when people confirm for themselves the promises made for them in infant baptism.

Raising children

One of the purposes of a Christian marriage is to have children and to bring them up in a secure Christian home. At a baptism, the congregation, parents and godparents all promise to introduce the baby to belief in God and encourage this as the child grows up. Christian parents do this because they believe that this is the way God intended us to live and it gives meaning and purpose to life.

Baptism

At baptism, the infant is introduced to the Church, the family of God, the godparents, friends and the congregation who promise to bring the infant up in the Christian faith and to be a good Christian example to the developing child.

Worship

The young child is taken to church on a regular basis. They are taught in a factual way important stories in Sunday School about Jesus, God and the early church. The majority of the people the young child meets believe in God and they all encourage the developing faith. The most memorable events in the young person's life will be the special occasions celebrated; these will usually be Christian festivals such as Christmas or Easter.

Adulthood

As the child grows into an adult, their Christian beliefs stay with them and are an integral part of their memories of happy, secure times. Should difficulties arise, the Christian community will be supportive through actions and prayer. It is from within the community in which they are established that they are likely to meet and marry someone who shares their beliefs. They then marry, have children and believe that a Christian upbringing offers children stability. They repeat the process and pass on their faith and beliefs. In the Bible it says, 'Bring a child up in the way he should go and he will not depart from it'.

Being part of the community

Churches often provide social events that bind the community and the family together. These may be prayer meetings, Bible study groups or purely social events such as youth clubs and parties to celebrate festivals. This sense of belonging helps the young person express their faith and build friendships with other people of their own age who believe in the same things. At this time, the world outside the family and community may begin to challenge what they believe.

School

Christian parents will often choose a Church school as this continues to surround their child with a strong sense of a community that all believe the same thing. The child will continue to be taught about the Christian faith and be encouraged to make a personal commitment to this in confirmation.

Activities

3   Read carefully the material in the five boxes outlining the features of a Christian upbringing shown on this spread. Then complete the boxes below.

Features of a religious upbringing	How these lead to or support belief in God

For discussion

- 'Parents should not force their religion onto their children.' Do you agree? Give reasons for your answer.
- How might Christian parents who attend church and believe in God avoid bringing up their children to believe in the same things as themselves? Is this possible?
- What other things might influence a person as they get older? Would these things affect their belief in God?

Summary

- Parents create an environment in which their children learn about God and see examples of how good Christians live.
- A Christian upbringing can establish a faith that lasts forever.

1.2 Religious experience and belief in God

Learning outcomes

By the end of this lesson you should be able to:

- give definitions for some of the key terms and use them in answers to questions
- outline and describe religious experiences
- give your own opinion about the validity of religious experiences, with evidence and reasons to support it
- explain how religious experience might lead to or support belief in God.

edexcel ⠿ key terms

Conversion – When your life is changed by giving yourself to God.

Miracle – Something that seems to break a law of science and makes you think only God could have done it.

Numinous – The feeling of the presence of something greater than you.

Prayer – An attempt to contact God, usually through words.

A personal encounter

Those people who do not have a Christian upbringing may come to believe in God for other reasons. Some people who are not Christian still have an association with Christianity because of things such as:

> A traditional belief that because I was born in what is called a Christian country I am a Christian.

> Things I have seen on television that give me general information about faith, for example on a TV drama or soap opera.

> We have the community celebration of festivals, for example Christmas.

> I had a chance meeting with a Christian, who told me about their faith.

These people may turn to the Church or pray to God for answers when they are having a difficult time. If they believe God responds to them, then they may come to a personal belief in God or strengthen their belief in God.

The most common religious experiences are a **miracle**, an answered **prayer** or a **numinous** experience.

Activities

1. Find an example of a miracle in the New Testament, read it and consider what the people around at the time may have said about the event. Imagine you were there. What would your response have been? Would it have led you to believe in God? Give reasons for your answer.

2. Describe one religious experience.

3. Explain how a religious experience might lead to, or encourage, belief in God.

Three girls experience a vision of the Virgin Mary in La Senora de Fatima *(1951).*

The main religious experiences

The religious experience	A description of it	How it may lead to or support belief in God
A miracle	This is something that happens that appears to break the laws of science and people attribute this event to God. Christians believe that the Old and New Testaments describe miracles performed by God. For Christians, Jesus's resurrection from the dead is the greatest miracle of all. Bernadette Soubirous had a vision of the Virgin Mary in Lourdes in 1858. Since then, many people have visited this place and have been healed because of their faith.	People who have experienced a miracle are convinced that only God could have done this. For them, this is evidence that God exists and it causes them either to believe in God or to strengthen their belief in God.
An answered prayer	Prayer is the personal way that Christians communicate with God. They may pray for an event or an intervention. An answered prayer is when the person praying believes that God has not only heard the prayer but has done as requested. For example, if someone is ill and prays to become well and then gets better.	This provides the person who prayed with the evidence that God exists (God must exist to have answered the prayer) and is also interested in them personally. This strengthens their faith.
A numinous experience	This is when something completely astonishes you. It is such an experience that words are not enough to describe the feeling, but it leaves you knowing that there must be something more powerful than you. Often people refer to things in the natural world that are so beautiful it overwhelms them, for example, the view from a mountain top. For others it may be an experience such as the birth of a baby.	For some people this experience is so powerful that it convinces them that God must exist.
Conversion	This is when someone who previously did not believe in God changes and begins to believe that God exists. A famous example would be that of St Paul on the road to Damascus. The converted person becomes suddenly aware of God and experiences a dramatic change of heart.	Conversion experiences often mean that a person is confronted with a choice – ultimately, whether to believe in God or not. The situation may occur in the form of an event or a person. However it comes about, the experience of conversion is a life-changing one.

ResultsPlus
Watch out!

Read the question slowly and carefully – some candidates have read conversion as conversation and given the wrong definition!

For discussion

Do you think God still performs miracles today? Give reasons for your answer.

Summary

Some people begin to believe in God through miracles, answered prayers, a numinous experience or a conversion experience, and these are used as evidence of God's existence.

1.3 Believing in God – and the design argument

Learning outcomes

By the end of this lesson you should be able to:

- outline the design argument
- explain how the design argument or the natural world could lead to or support belief in God
- give your own opinion, with reasons, about the validity of the design argument and its links to belief in God.

The design argument and belief in God

People have always enjoyed designing things. They have taken things and put them together in a variety of ways to come up with new objects either to make the world prettier or to make life easier. Designing artefacts takes time and effort, plans are drawn up and ideas are made into reality. It is not often that something useful occurs simply by accident.

Activities

1 In your Design and Technology Department in school things are planned, designed and made. What was the most recent thing you designed and made? Describe the process you went through to create your masterpiece.

2 How would you feel if someone came along and said that your creation was just an accident and that you didn't contribute to it? It was just something that happened by itself.

This sculpture is called 'The Tree of Life'. It is part of an art project that took guns off the streets of Mozambique and used them to design symbols of peace. Four artists spent several years planning the work and deciding how best to use the guns to create a sculpture.

For discussion

When you look at the sculpture 'The Tree of Life' would you assume that it had a designer? Why, or why not?

Many people believe that the world and the universe were designed. They did not come about just by accident or through a 'big bang', but were designed and made by God.

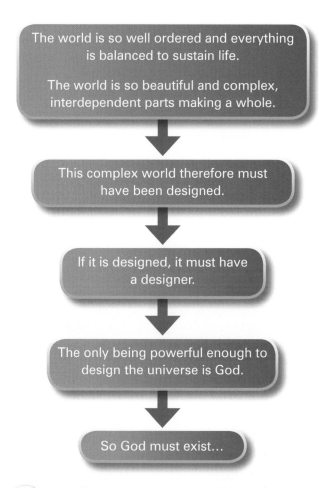

The world is so well ordered and everything is balanced to sustain life.

The world is so beautiful and complex, interdependent parts making a whole.

↓

This complex world therefore must have been designed.

↓

If it is designed, it must have a designer.

↓

The only being powerful enough to design the universe is God.

↓

So God must exist…

For discussion

'All creation is an outstretched finger pointing to God.' Do you agree? Give reasons for your answer.

Paley's watch

A famous philosopher, William Paley, made an analogy between the watch and the world, both of which have complex and distinctive features. He said that if someone found a watch (an old-fashioned watch with cogs and wheels inside) and had never seen one before in their lives, they would be curious and amazed. They would naturally assume that something that was so carefully made and dependent on all the correct pieces being in the right place at the right time must have been designed and created by a very clever person. Paley argued that the same could be said of the universe, which is much more complicated. It could never have happened by chance, it must have had a clever designer and powerful creator. The only possible being capable of this was God. Therefore, he concluded, God exists.

Many people think that how scientists understand DNA is the most important discovery of the last hundred years. DNA was discovered, scientists did not create it, but they are amazed by it.

For discussion

Could something as complex as DNA have happened by accident?

If these accidents created life, why do we not see accidents that create life today or unique 'natural' happenings?

Activities

3 Outline the design argument.

4 Explain how the natural world might lead someone to believe in God.

Summary

Some people argue that the complexity of the natural world and the uniqueness of a person's DNA and thumbprint support belief in God.

1.4 Believing in God – and the causation argument

Learning outcomes

By the end of this lesson you should be able to:

- outline the argument for believing in God based on causation
- explain how the causation argument can lead to or support belief in God
- give examples of things that have a cause in the universe and express your opinion on whether the causation argument should convince people of the existence of God.

Activities

1 Watch one news programme. For each news item identify who is to be blamed or praised for the event being reported. In each case this will be the 'cause' of what has happened.

As with these dominoes, in a chain of events one thing causes another.

For discussion

Do you think things can happen by chance? Give an example of something that happens without a cause.

In our world, especially in classrooms, you can often hear the cry, 'It's not my fault. I didn't cause it!' There seems to be an understanding that when things happen someone or something must be responsible. This allows us to blame people for the bad things that happen and to celebrate the cause of the good things that happen.

When it comes to the creation of the world and evidence that God exists, some people use similar arguments. They argue that nothing happens by chance – everything has a reason or a cause. This is known as causation.

The argument develops logically.

Watch out!

Many candidates confuse the argument from causation with the design argument. Make sure that you know the differences between the two!

A medieval Christian thinker called Thomas Aquinas wrote:

> In the cosmos as we experience it, it is obvious to us that some things change. Now, whatever changes must have been changed by something else. And if that something else in turn changes then it must have been changed by another. But this cannot go on to infinity… you eventually have to arrive at something that is unchanging. This is God!

Activities

2 Look at the words of Thomas Aquinas on page 10. What does he mean?

3 What is your opinion about what he said? Give your reasons.

4 Explain how this argument could convince people to believe in God.

The logic behind the causation argument appears to prove God's existence. However, the final step in the argument still requires belief in a superior being who caused the universe and some people find this hard to accept.

Activities

5 List reasons to agree with the causation argument (its strengths) and reasons to disagree with this argument (its weaknesses). What is your opinion of both sides of the argument and what reasons would you give to support your thoughts?

6 Turn your notes into a piece of writing that reflects both sides of the argument and concludes with your thoughts, giving reasons.

Nothing can happen by itself

↓

Everything that happens must be caused by something else

↓

The universe could not have 'just happened' by itself

↓

A very powerful force must have caused the universe

↓

This cause must have been God

↓

This means God must exist

ResultsPlus
Top tip!

You may be asked to answer: 'Do you think that God was the cause of the universe?' Give **two** reasons for your answer. The word 'caused' should prompt you to think 'causation argument'! You can use the causation argument to explain what you think.

For this question you must give **two** reasons and explain how these support your point of view.

You may also be asked 'Do you think that God designed the universe?' or 'Do you think that God created the universe?'

Summary

Some people argue that everything in the world has a cause and therefore the world must have a cause – and that cause is God.

1.5 Scientific explanations of the origins of the world and belief in God

Learning outcomes

By the end of this lesson you should be able to:

- outline why some people do not believe in God
- outline the scientific explanations of the origins of the world
- explain why scientific explanations of the origins of the world may lead some people to doubt the existence of God
- evaluate the different arguments given and express your own response to the scientific explanations of the world, giving reasons and evidence for your opinion, and showing you understand the alternative point of view.

edexcel ⠿ key terms

Agnosticism – Not being sure whether God exists.

Atheism – Believing that God does not exist.

Non-belief in God

Some people do not believe in God. They are called atheists and not believing in God is **atheism**. Other people are unsure about what to believe and claim we cannot know whether God exists or not. These people are called agnostics and not being sure that God exists is **agnosticism**.

For people who do not believe in God, there appear to be other explanations about the origins of the world rather than those of design or causation.

Activities

1 Make a chart with two columns. In the first column, write a list of the reasons why some people believe in God. Use the material you have already studied. In the second column give a reason why someone might not believe in God.

One of the most popular scientific theories is the 'big bang'. In its simplest form, this is the idea that an explosion of matter took place about 15 billion years ago and, from this explosion, the world came into being, and continues to expand and evolve without involvement from any outside power.

For discussion

'Animals still evolve and adapt to their environments, which proves that God did not create them.' Do you agree? Give reasons for your answer.

Charles Darwin, after studying animals and insect life from different countries, came to the conclusion that all living things had evolved over a period of time to suit the environment in which they found themselves. Each generation of animal therefore improved and evolved to survive. According to modern scientists, apes have common genetic material with human beings, and this indicates that humans evolved from apes. Darwin's theory suggests that God did not create all life uniquely but rather it evolved from one source.

Activities

2 Outline the scientific explanation for the origins of the world.

3 Explain why this may cause some people to doubt God's existence.

Activities

4 Look at these photos of living beings. Which is the odd one out? Why? What do they all have in common? Which do you think came first? Put them in evolutionary order.

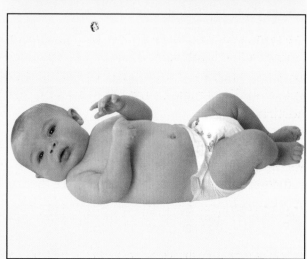

One of the key reasons that these theories lead people to doubt God's existence is because they are supported by evidence that can be seen and tested. For example, fossils have been found that show the development of some animals into more complex forms. Scientists acknowledge that, at the moment, theories about the origin of the world cannot be totally explained by science but claim that they will be in the future.

Summary

- Some people do not believe in God (atheists) and others are not sure (agnostics).
- Many atheists do not believe in God because they believe that science can account for the creation of the world and the animals on it.

1.6 How Christians respond to the scientific explanations of the world

14

Learning outcomes

By the end of this lesson you should be able to:

- give a definition of the word omnipotent
- describe the different Christian responses to the scientific explanations of the universe
- evaluate the different arguments given and express your own response to the scientific explanations of the universe, giving reasons and evidence for your opinion, and showing that you understand the alternative point of view.

edexcel ::: key terms

Omnipotent – The belief that God is all-powerful.

Other Christians

Some Christians

Christian responses

When someone presents an argument against God, with reasons and evidence, Christians have to respond to it. They must weigh up the information presented and suggest ways in which this information does not challenge their faith in a supreme God. When presented with the scientific explanations of the origins of the world, Christians respond in different ways.

Some Christians reject the scientific explanations. They argue that the accounts of creation in Genesis are the truth and can be supported by faith and evidence.

For discussion

Ask yourself the following questions:

- What would you regard as evidence of God's existence?
- What, for you, would be the ultimate proof that God exists?
- Can God be detected, and if so, how?
- What sort of instrument would be suitable to detect God?

Some Christians believe that the Bible is fact; they think it is true in every way. These Christians are called fundamentalists. They believe that the world was created by an **omnipotent** God in six days.

Other Christians believe the Bible can be interpreted and that the message and meaning are true, but that some stories in the Bible are meant to represent a greater truth and are not actually what happened. They accept that science tells us how the world came into being, but the Bible tells us why it came into being. In some cases, they say that the six days are symbolic of six ages in the process of creation.

Some Christians believe that the physical form of the world can be explained without God, but the beauty within it cannot. The world is so beautiful and mysterious that there must have been a power behind its beginning, and that must be God.

ResultsPlus
Watch out!

When you are considering your own point of view, remember that you need reasons for it. To gain full marks you need to recognise what people who disagree with you think and what reasons they would give for that point of view.

Activities

1 The atheist Richard Dawkins supports Darwin's theory. Look up his work and ideas on the Internet and write a short explanation of why he does not believe in God. He uses the phrase 'purpose coloured spectacles'. What do you think this means?

For discussion

- What is the most important question: How did we get here? Why are we here?
- Even if everything did evolve, surely for the world to be so full of beautiful things there must have been some greater plan?

Activities

2 On small pieces of paper write down the different explanations from the last few chapters about the origins of the world, Christian and scientific (your teacher may have a photocopy for you to cut up).

- In pairs, spend time discussing each point of view and create a hierarchy of arguments, the one you are most convinced by at the top.
- Take the argument you most strongly agree with and give two reasons why you do so.
- Take the argument you are the least convinced by and give two reasons why someone might hold this point of view.

Summary

- Some Christians believe that the Bible account of creation is true and reject the scientific explanations.
- Others believe that there is no conflict between the Bible and science, and that the creation story can be seen in the scientific evidence and six days equals six ages.
- Some Christians believe that the physical form of the world can be experienced without God, but the beauty within it cannot. The world is so beautiful and mysterious that there must have been a power behind its beginning, and that must be God.

1.7 Unanswered prayers, non-belief in God and the Christian response

16

Learning outcomes

By the end of this lesson you will be able to:

- describe what is meant by unanswered prayers
- explain how this might make someone doubt or reject the existence of God
- express your opinion on whether prayers are answered or not and explain why this encourages you to believe or not believe in God.

edexcel ▦ key terms

Omni-benevolent – The belief that God is all-good.

Omniscient – The belief that God knows everything that has happened and everything that will happen.

Unanswered prayers

Atheists are confident that if God existed, and was **omni-benevolent** and **omniscient**, then surely everyone's prayers would be answered. Many people experience suffering and pain in their lives or watch as family and friends suffer, and God seems to do nothing. This makes it easy for some people to reject belief in God. They see millions of people praying for the same thing all over the world, such as world peace, and God does nothing.

Even for Christians, the fact that God appears not to answer prayers can cause a problem for them. It may lead to doubt and a testing of their faith in God.

For discussion

Do you think God should answer all prayers? Give reasons for your answer.

Christian responses

Christians have to respond to this challenge. Some Christians accept that God hears and answers all prayers, but sometimes the answer is 'no', or 'not now'. Christians believe that they have to trust God to do what is best for them. Other Christians believe that God may have answered the prayer but not in the way that was expected or hoped for. They believe that God has an ultimate plan for

each person and will respond to prayers that fit into that plan. Some prayers will contradict other people's prayers and therefore God cannot answer these prayers at the same time.

In the film Bruce Almighty *when Bruce, acting as God, said 'yes' to all prayers there were riots and society became chaotic.*

Activities

1 In the film *Bruce Almighty* when Bruce, acting as God, said 'yes' to all prayers there were riots and society became chaotic. Why do you think this would happen?

2 What types of prayer might God choose not to answer? Why?

3 When people face extreme difficulties they often pray. Why do you think this is so? Do you think God should answer prayers from people who do not follow Christianity carefully?

4 What do you think about the response of Christians to unanswered prayers?

5 Have you ever prayed? What for? Was it answered?

6 If God answered your prayer would you believe in him? Or would you find another explanation for what had happened?

ResultsPlus
Build better answers

'Unanswered prayers prove that God does not exist.'
(i) Do you agree? Give reasons for your opinion.
(3 marks)

 Basic, 1-mark answers
These answers would offer a simple opinion with a reason. Be aware of the difference between saying what you think, and giving reasons why you think it.

 Good, 2-mark answers
Answers that receive two marks would either offer two reasons for their opinion or one well-developed reason. This means that you say something extra to explain your reason.

 Excellent, 3-mark answers
The best answers would either give three simple reasons, or two reasons with some explanation or evidence, or a fully developed explanation of how the reasons support the opinion.

(ii) Give reasons why some people will disagree with you. (3 marks)

 Basic, 1-mark answers
These answers would offer a simple opinion with a reason.

 Good, 2-mark answers
These answers either offer one reason that is well-explained or two simple reasons.

▲ **Excellent, 3-mark answers**
The best answers would either give three simple reasons, or two reasons with some explanation or evidence, or a fully developed explanation of how the reasons support the opinion.

Summary

• Some people believe that the fact that not all prayers are answered proves that there is no God.

• Christians respond to this in a variety of ways and believe that they have to trust that God knows what he is doing.

1.8 Evil, suffering and belief in God

Learning outcomes

By the end of this lesson, you will be able to:

● explain what evil is and how this might cause suffering

● describe the problem of evil and suffering for Christians

● explain why the existence of evil and suffering in the world might cause someone to doubt or reject belief in God

● give your own opinion of what suffering is, with reasons.

edexcel ⠿ key terms

Moral evil – Actions done by humans which cause suffering.

Natural evil – Things which cause suffering but have nothing to do with humans.

What is suffering?

Heather believes she is suffering. She understands that, to other people, her suffering is minor. It is not life-threatening like the people suffering in the famine shown on TV, or the floods that have left them homeless. Nevertheless, her suffering is real to her. It's not her fault that she has never needed food, shelter or clothing. That is just the way life has happened to her. However, last night her parents took away her mobile phone and hair straighteners. She feels devastated and isolated. She cannot stop crying and cannot imagine carrying on without her phone. She is frightened of being seen. She sits alone in her room wondering when it will end...

For discussion

● Can you identify with Heather's suffering? Is it less important than someone else's suffering?

● Do we need suffering to make us appreciate the things we have?

Natural and moral evil

Everyone in life experiences things that cause them to suffer, from stubbing their toe to watching a loved one die. This appears to be part of life. Many people link suffering and evil together – suffering is what happens after an act of evil.

This selection of pictures shows examples of evil and suffering. What is evil?

Activity

1 Write a list of 10 'evil' things and divide them into natural and moral evil.
   - With a partner choose five of the most evil things on your lists.
   - Put these in order: the most evil is...; the least evil is...
   - As you do this, discuss why one thing is more evil than another. Make a note of the reasons you have put these things in this order.
   - Compare your list with the rest of the class.

There are two main types of evil. **Natural evil** refers to suffering that is caused by nature, for example, an earthquake. **Moral evil** is suffering caused by human beings.

The existence of evil and suffering causes problems for Christians and it is often said to be the strongest argument against the existence of God.

It can be outlined in this way.

God is:

> An omni-benevolent God would not want people to suffer and would remove the causes of suffering.

- omni-benevolent
- omnipotent
- omniscient.

> An omnipotent God would be able to remove the causes of suffering.

> An omniscient God would know how to remove the causes of suffering.

Either God is not omni-benevolent, omnipotent or omniscient, or God does not exist.

Evil and suffering do exist, therefore God cannot.

For discussion

- Is it possible to say that God does exist, but may not be as we imagined? Might the story of Noah's Ark tell us that God does not always behave as we would expect?
- Some people claim that there is no such thing as evil. It is just the absence of good. As darkness does not exist, it is just the absence of light. What do you think about this idea?
- In many stories and films, when good and evil battle good always wins. Why do you think this is so?
- Does the suffering of others remind us that we are not suffering?

Summary

- All people suffer in various ways.
- Moral evil and natural evil are present in the world.
- The presence of evil and suffering in the world causes some people to doubt God's existence.

1.9 Christian responses to evil and suffering

A variety of Christian responses

The problem of evil and suffering sets a challenge to Christian beliefs about God. Christians believe that God is omni-benevolent, omnipotent and omniscient, but allows suffering to happen. God even allows suffering to happen to people who believe and follow his teachings and to those who are innocent. How can that be?

A victim of the Asian tsunami.

edexcel **key terms**

Free will – The idea that human beings are free to make their own choices.

Reasons for evil and suffering

Christian response	Explanation
It was planned from the beginning of time after Adam and Eve disobeyed God.	God created a perfect world, but Adam and Eve chose to disobey God. Their punishment was separation from God. This led to suffering and evil. God's plan then involved sending Jesus to restore the relationship and save humanity.
Evil and suffering is a test from God.	God is testing believers as to how they may react. Some may reject God, others may grow closer to God and try to become stronger, more loving and patient characters. The result of the test determines the afterlife.
Evil is not God's fault – humans have **free will**.	We are not programmed like computers and therefore can choose evil and then suffering occurs. Suffering is a result of our choices in life.
God knows why these things happen but we cannot.	God's ultimate plan may need to be brought about by suffering. God has the answer and we have not. We must trust God.
It allows us to follow Jesus's example.	Jesus taught believers the need for prayer and good works. Without suffering we cannot do this. (Matthew 25: 35–36, 40)

Activities

1   Write a letter to someone who is suffering. Explain to them, from a Christian point of view, how this is not God's fault.

2   In what ways could Christians put their faith into action and help those who suffer?

3   Can God be omnipotent if we have free will?

ResultsPlus
Exam question report

Explain how Christians respond to the problem of evil and suffering. (8 marks) June 2007

How students answered

The candidates who scored poorly on this question answered generally about the problem of evil and suffering rather than explaining how Christians respond to it.

Most of the candidates who scored 3–6 marks for this question explained one Christian response to the problem of evil, such as a test from God.

There were some excellent answers that gave a detailed response to at least two of the different ways in which Christians deal with the problem of evil and suffering.

For discussion

'Good always comes out of evil.' Do you agree? Give reasons.

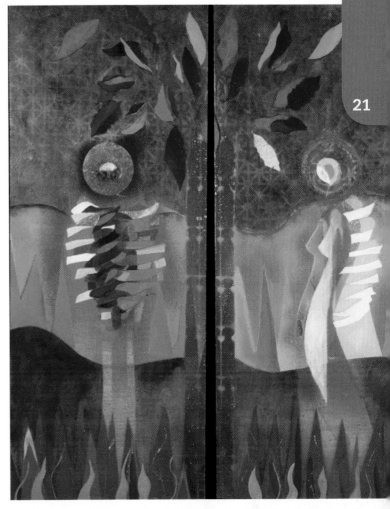

Genesis says that Adam and Eve chose to disobey God, and their punishment was separation from God.

Summary

- Christians attempt to solve the problem of evil by explaining why God permits evil and suffering even though an omnipotent God could remove it.

- Some Christians argue that evil and suffering is a test from God in order to draw people near to God.

- Other Christians use the Bible (Genesis 1–3) to explain how suffering came into the world through human exercise of their free will.

1.10 The media and belief in God

Learning outcomes

By the end of this lesson you should be able to:

- describe two programmes that could affect a person's attitude towards belief in God
- explain how either of these programmes might affect a person's attitude to belief in God
- evaluate the positive and negative messages sent through the media about belief in God and express your opinion on this, with reasons and evidence.

Glossary

Programmes about religion – These are programmes where religion is the main feature or way of presenting an idea or story.

TV programmes

When viewers discuss a TV programme, it can sound as if the characters are real and a part of our lives. People come to know them, as if they are friends, and have a unique glimpse into their lives, sharing with them the joy and distress of the events that take place. This may be over a period of weeks with a soap opera or for a shorter time in the case of a drama or radio programme.

For discussion

TV programmes can have a powerful effect on people's lives and their attitudes. Why do you think this is so?

In your lessons, your teacher will show you two examples of TV programmes, radio programmes or films that could influence a person's belief in God. During this section we have given some examples of films and dramas, and suggested that you look at newspaper reports. You may use these examples to support your answers in any media question.

Impact of the media

The media can influence our attitudes by presenting ideas as if they are facts, or facts as if they are fiction. When it comes to 'belief in God', some programmes give a message to viewers that having faith and believing in God is positive and should be embraced or encouraged, and that it can be beneficial. There are some specifically religious programmes that are designed to support belief in God and enable the viewer to feel part of a religious community.

Other programmes may make belief in God appear humorous or ridiculous. They present people who believe in God as bizarre and slightly strange, and encourage the viewer to share this attitude towards belief in God.

Activities

1 Which of these TV programmes is the odd one out?

2 For each programme, say how it could influence a person's belief in God.

3 List the programmes you watch or listen to (on the radio), and films or dramas you have seen on TV that have some religious content that could affect a person's attitude towards belief in God.

4 Compare your list with a friend and put the two lists together.

5 Choose two programmes from your combined list. Place them in the centre of a piece of paper. Around them, write the positive and negative messages given by this programme about belief in God.

6 Do you think that these messages would be received by other viewers?

Songs of Praise

Father Ted

The Vicar of Dibley

Life in Cold Blood

I think everyone should be able to choose if they believe in God or not, I can make my own mind up without help from the TV!

I wouldn't believe in God! They are all bizarre. Have you seen the congregation in *The Vicar of Dibley*?

For discussion

● How much does what you see on TV or hear on the radio affect your attitude to belief in God?

● Can other programmes, such as David Attenborough's *Life in Cold Blood*, which inspires awe and wonder in the natural world as it developed through the evolutionary process, cause someone to believe in God? Explain why.

Summary

● The broadcast media (TV and radio) show many programmes that portray people believing in God.

● This can influence people's attitudes towards belief in God.

Quick quiz

1 What does the word omnipotent mean?

2 What does the word numinous mean?

3 Explain how a religious upbringing might lead to or support belief in God. Describe one religious experience.

4 Outline the argument for believing in God based on causation.

5 Outline the argument for believing in God based on design.

6 Explain how Christians respond to the problem of evil and suffering.

7 Do you think the world was created by God? Give two reasons for your answer.

8 Do you think God should answer all prayers? Give two reasons for your answer.

9 Explain why some people do not believe in God.

Plenary activity

Create two characters, of any age, gender, race, background or circumstances. One of them is an atheist, the other is a theist (believer in God). Using all the material in this section, write a short report about each character, filling in their personal details as suggested above, and explaining what they believe. For example, you could create a character named Alan, who is in his mid-30s, brought up in a Christian home, but who now describes himself as an atheist. Why has he stopped believing in God? Did he ever believe? What does he think about suffering in the world, prayer, the possible causes for the origin of the world, and so on?

Try to get into the minds of these characters so that they feel real to you and to someone who might read your account. Help the reader to understand why your characters truly hold their beliefs. Try to include in each character's story something from every lesson in this section.

Find out more

Channel Four television shows many programmes that deal with key issues of religious belief, such as those described in this section. Keep an eye on their website for programmes that may help with your course. Go to www.heinemann.co.uk/hotlinks (express code 4202P) and click on the appropriate link.

You could record some programmes and watch others. These programmes will give you a better idea of how important religion is to people all over the world, whether people believe in God themselves or not.

Take the opportunity to pick up leaflets in churches and other places of worship or where Christians meet together. These will often deal with questions people have about faith, or they may advertise events going on there or nearby that could give you a greater insight into why people believe and what they do together.

Many churches run Alpha courses, which teach the fundamentals of the Christian faith. Go to www.heinemann.co.uk/hotlinks (express code 4202P) and click on the appropriate link.

Student tips

When I studied these topics for my GCSE, I made sure that I knew all the key terms very well. This was so I could be sure of getting full marks for all the questions that asked for meanings of key terms, but also so I could use some of them in other answers to show my understanding of the topics. For example, I could use 'omnipotent' when writing about why religious believers have to find solutions to the problem of evil, even if there wasn't a short question that asked what that word means.

Self-evaluation checklist

Look at the following table. How would you rate your understanding of this topic? Use the following code to judge your status:

Green – I understand this fully.
Orange – I am confident I can answer most questions on this.
Red – I need to do a lot more work on this topic.

Now answer the following questions:

- Do you hold an opinion on this topic and could you give reasons for that opinion if asked?
- Can you give the opinion of someone who disagrees with you and give reasons they hold this opinion?

Content covered	My understanding is red/orange/ green	Can I give my opinion?	Can I give an alternative opinion?
The main features of a Christian upbringing.			
How a Christian upbringing may lead to or support belief in God.			
Religious experiences such as numinous, conversion, miracles and prayer.			
How a religious experience may lead to or support belief in God.			
The argument from causation.			
The argument from design.			
How the arguments from design and causation may or may not lead to belief in God.			
Why scientific explanations of the origins of the world may lead some people to reject belief in God.			
How Christians respond to the scientific explanations of the world.			
Why unanswered prayers may lead some people to reject belief in God.			
How Christians respond to the problem of unanswered prayers.			
Why evil and suffering may lead some people to reject belief in God.			
How Christians respond to the problem of evil and suffering.			
How two television programmes and/or radio programmes and/or films about religion may affect a person's attitude to belief in God.			

Introduction

In the exam you will see a choice of two questions on this module. Each question will include four tasks, which test your knowledge, understanding and evaluation of the material covered. A 2-mark question will ask you to define a term; a 4-mark question will ask your opinion on a point of view; an 8-mark question will ask you to explain a particular belief or idea; a 6-mark question will ask for your opinion on a point of view and ask you to consider an alternative point of view.

Give a glossary definition. You do not need to write any more – often this can be done in one sentence.

The 'explain how' questions are asking you to connect two things and show how they are related to each other. In this case how the (1) religious upbringing, connects to (2) belief in God. Therefore, if you only describe a religious upbringing you can only achieve level one. You have to break down the features of a religious upbringing and say how each one leads to belief in God. Once the examiner has awarded the level for your answer, they will look at the quality of your spelling and punctuation, and use this to decide if you gain 7 or 8 marks. Be aware on the C questions to use formal English and check your spellings etc.

Mini exam paper

(a) What is **atheism**? (2 marks)

(b) Do you think prayer is a waste of time?
    Give **two** reasons for your point of view. (4 marks)

(c) Explain how a religious upbringing may lead to belief in God. (8 marks)

(d) *'Evil and suffering prove that God does not exist.'*
    In your answer you should refer to at least one religion.
    (i) Do you agree? Give reasons for your opinion. (3 marks)
    (ii) Give reasons why some people may disagree with you. (3 marks)

Give your opinion. Note, however, that marks are only awarded for the reasons you have for thinking that opinion is correct. Each reason needs to be explained to gain the marks available. For example, on this example one reason would be 'It's a way to contact God.' This would get 1 mark. To increase it to 2 marks it needs to be developed – for example, 'It's a way to contact God which helps to make you a better Christian.' You can get no more marks for one reason; to move on to 3 and 4 marks you have to give a second reason.

The (d) question is split into two parts – answer each part separately. You must refer to the statement and Christian beliefs during this whole question. It may be worth considering whether Christians would agree or disagree with this statement and use their reasons in (ii) and then provide the alternative point of view as your own.

(i) You must give one very well explained reason for your opinion or three simple reasons to gain full marks.

(ii) You must now show you understand the reasons that someone might disagree with you.

Mark scheme

(a) You will earn **2 marks** for a correct answer, and **1 mark** for a partially correct answer.

(b) To earn up to the full **4 marks** you need to give two reasons (as asked) and to develop them fully. Two brief reasons will earn **2 marks** and one reason without development will earn **1 mark**.

(c) You can earn **7–8 marks** by giving up to four reasons, but the fewer reasons you give, the more you must develop them. You are being assessed on your use of language, so you also need to take care to express your understanding in a clear style of English, and to make some use of specialist vocabulary.

(d) To go beyond **3 marks** for the whole of this question you must refer to Christianity. The more you are able to develop your reasons the more marks you will earn. Three simple reasons can earn you the same mark as one fully developed reason.

ResultsPlus
Maximise your marks

(b) Do you think prayer is a waste of time? Give **two** reasons for your point of view. (4 marks)

Student answer	Examiner comments	Improved student answer
I think that prayer is not a waste of time as it is a way to make contact with God. Even though God cannot be seen or heard in the usual way, believers in God can speak to him through prayer and believe that he is listening.	It is important to give TWO clear reasons for your opinion. It is better to identify your reasons with the word 'because' and say why you think something not just what you think. In this answer the student says 'it is a way to contact God', giving 1 mark. The next sentence develops this, giving 2 marks.	I think prayer is not a waste of time because it is a way to make contact with God. Even though God cannot be seen or heard in the usual way, believers still find comfort in talking to him.
There is always the chance that he may answer the believer's prayer and make their lives better.	The next reason given is that it can make believers live better, but the student does not explain how or why this would happen, gaining only another mark. In total, this answer would be likely to gain 3 marks.	I also think it is not a waste of time because when a person prays for someone it is a way of showing your love or concern for them. It can make you feel as if you have done something to help, especially at times when you can do nothing else.

Matters of life and death

Introduction

In this section you will learn about major issues that concern everyone, not only religious believers – issues of life and death. We will all die at some point but for religious believers what happens after death is crucially important, and so is how we deal with life on Earth. How highly do we value life and what steps do we take to improve it and protect it? In this section you will learn how Christians go about answering these questions.

> ### Learning outcomes for this section
>
> By the end of this section you will be able to:
>
> - give definitions of the key terms and use them in answers to GCSE questions
> - explain why Christians believe in life after death and how these beliefs affect the way they live their lives
> - outline non-religious reasons for believing in life after death (near-death experiences, ghosts, mediums, evidence of reincarnation)
> - explain why some people do not believe in life after death
> - outline the current law on abortion in the United Kingdom and explain why abortion is a controversial issue
> - describe different Christian attitudes to abortion and explain why there are differences
> - outline the current law on euthanasia in the United Kingdom and explain why euthanasia is a controversial issue
> - describe different Christian attitudes to euthanasia and explain why there are differences
> - describe the causes of world poverty
> - explain how and why one Christian agency is trying to end world poverty
> - give arguments for and against the media being free to criticise what religions say about matters of life and death
> - describe how an issue raised in this section (abortion, euthanasia, life after death or poverty) has been presented in the media.

edexcel ::: key terms

abortion	**immortality of the soul**	**paranormal**	**resurrection**
assisted suicide	**near-death experience**	**quality of life**	**sanctity of life**
euthanasia	**non-voluntary euthanasia**	**reincarnation**	**voluntary euthanasia**

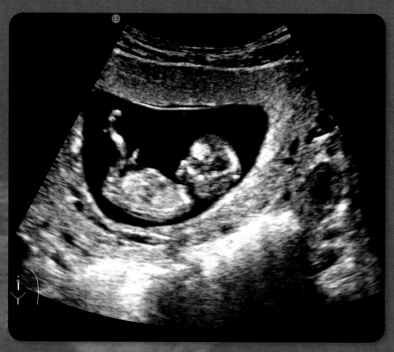

When does life begin?

Is it ever right to kill?

What happens to you when you die?

Work in pairs to answer the questions posed by the images.

Look carefully at your answers. People might ask you to provide reasons and evidence for your opinion. List the questions they might ask you. For example, if you said 'Life begins at birth', when did the 'being' begin to have the potential to be a human being? Does this make them alive? What is life? Is life given by God?

Keep these questions and answers safe for the rest of the section to refer to when you are asked for your own opinion.

Fascinating fact

According to Benjamin Franklin (1789), 'In this world, nothing is certain but death and taxes.'

2.1 Why Christians believe in life after death

Learning outcomes

By the end of this lesson, you should be able to:

- give definitions of the key terms
- explain why Christians believe in life after death
- give your own opinion on life after death, stating what you believe happens when we die, giving reasons and evidence for your opinion.

edexcel ⠿ key terms

Paranormal – Unexplained things which are thought to have spiritual causes, e.g. ghosts or mediums.

Life after death

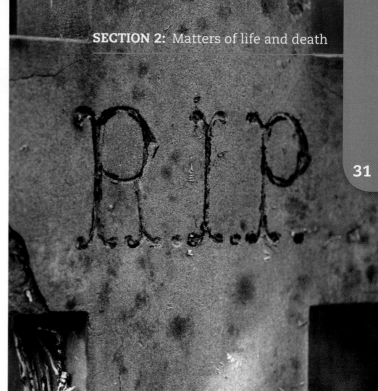

Activities

1 Consider what each of these images says about life after death. Which one is the closest representation to your own belief about life after death?

2 Create your own picture, expressing your feelings about death and the afterlife. It could be a symbolic collection of colours and words or just a simple drawing. Write a short explanation of how you came to your final design.

3 For those who believe in life after death, what is it that lives on?

Why Christians believe in life after death

All Christians believe in life after death. They believe in life after death because:

● The basis of Christianity is that Jesus rose from the dead which suggests there is an afterlife for everyone.
● There are many verses in the Bible which mention the afterlife.
● The Christian Churches all teach that there is life after death.
● It is part of the Creeds of the Churches.
● Some Christians believe they have experienced the **paranormal**.
● It gives life meaning and purpose.

Although Christians all believe in an afterlife, they have different view on what happens when people die. Most believe in immortality of the soul or the resurrection of the body. We will look at this in more detail on page 32.

ResultsPlus
Watch out!

If you are asked to explain why Christians believe in life after death you do not have to say what they believe happens. This will not be given any marks.

Activities

4 Explain why Christians believe in life after death.

5 Do you believe in the paranormal? Give reasons for your answer.

Summary

● People have many different views about what happens after death.
● All Christians believe in life after death because of the teachings of the Bible and the Church and because they believe that Jesus rose from death.

2.2 How Christian beliefs about life after death affect the way they live

Learning outcomes

By the end of the lesson you should be able to:

- describe the different beliefs about life after death in Christianity
- explain why there are different beliefs about life after death in Christianity
- explain how the belief in life after death affects the way Christians live.

edexcel ⠿ key terms

Immortality of the soul – The idea that the soul lives on after the death of the body.

Resurrection – The belief that, after death, the body stays in the grave until the end of the world when it is raised.

Christian beliefs in life after death

Who	Believes what	Why
Many Protestant Christians	Believe that after death the body will stay in the grave, but the soul will go straight to God for judgement. There is a difference of opinion about what will happen to those who do not go to Heaven, and some believe there is no such place as Hell.	• Jesus told a thief on the cross that he would be in Heaven that day (Luke 23:43). • Jesus said his father's house had many rooms that Jesus was preparing for his followers (John 14:2). • The teaching of the Church is that there can be a communion of the saints (communication between dead and living Christians). • Evidence of the paranormal such as ghosts and mediums.
Other evangelical Protestant Christians	Believe that after death the body and soul stay in the grave until the end of the world. At this time a Christian will be judged. The good will go to Heaven and sinners who have not repented will go to Hell.	• Jesus's body was raised from the dead (Luke 24:39). • They are taught to believe in the resurrection of the body and everlasting life. • St Paul teaches this belief in 1 Corinthians 15:42–44.
Roman Catholic Christians	Believe in both the resurrection of the body and immortality of the soul. They believe that the soul of a Christian who has not sinned since their last confession will go straight to Heaven. The soul of a Christian that has sinned will go to Purgatory for their souls to be cleansed. The souls who do not believe in God or have committed unforgivable sins will go to Hell. After this, Jesus will come back to Earth to raise the dead and reunite their bodies and souls. God will make a new Heaven and a new Earth and the souls in Purgatory will go to Heaven and the souls from Hell will return to Hell.	• The resurrection of Jesus. • The teachings of the New Testament. • The teaching in the Catechism of the Catholic Church. • They believe that Jesus is seated on the right hand of the father and will come again to judge the living and the dead.

Activities

1   If you were to add your opinion at the end of this chart, what would it be?
2   Explain different Christian beliefs in life after death.
3   Explain how these beliefs affect the way that Christians live their lives.

Christians have different views on what happens when you die. Most believe in **immortality of the soul** or the **resurrection** of the body.

The effect on Christians' lives

The belief in life after death affects the way Christians live their lives.

- Christians believe that they will be judged by God after death, so they live within the guidelines given in the Bible and by the Church. This affects how they live their lives and how they treat others.

- The fact that Jesus rose from the dead gives them hope that they will also rise, and that in the afterlife they will be rewarded for their time on Earth.

- The promise of the afterlife means forgiveness for some Christians who have done awful things but repented and now hope for a better future.

- It offers comfort to those who have suffered the death of a loved one.

Some Christians say that the promise of Heaven is more important because of the quality of life they have now in preparation for that day.

For discussion

'It is steak on your plate, while you wait. Not pie in the sky when you die.' What do you think this means? Do you agree with this statement? Give reasons for your answer.

Summary

- There is a variety of Christian views about what happens. Most Christians believe in either the immortality of the soul or the resurrection of the body.
- This affects how Christians live their lives because they believe God will reward those who have lived according to God's will.

2.3 Why some non-religious people believe in life after death

Learning outcomes

By the end of this lesson, you should be able to:

- explain why some non-religious people believe in life after death
- explain why some non-religious people reject the belief in life after death
- describe one example of media that covers an issue from this section
- evaluate whether the treatment of the theme was fair to religious beliefs or people
- give your own point of view, with reasons.

edexcel ::: key terms

Near-death experience – When somebody about to die has an out of body experience.

Reincarnation – The belief that, after death, souls are reborn in a new body.

Why some non-religious people believe in life after death

Many people who do not believe in God and consider themselves atheist or agnostic still believe in life after death. It would appear that most people, whether they are religious or not, need to feel that this life is not just all there is. There is an increasing interest in mediums and ghost hunting.

Near-death experiences

Near-death experiences have been reported by patients who have been pronounced dead for a short period of time. They describe leaving their bodies and seeing themselves from outside their body. In some cases, they report seeing relatives and friends who have already died or a bright light they feel they want to travel towards. They are convinced that this is evidence there is an afterlife.

Ghosts

These are thought to be the spirits of dead people who, for some reason, have not travelled on to the 'next place'.

They can be experienced as a physical presence that is seen or as the sense or feeling of someone being with you. It is believed that some ghosts may haunt the living, while others come to support and look after loved ones or to try and contact the living.

Some people claim to have experienced the paranormal.

Contacting the dead

People such as mediums claim to be able to contact the dead. Contacting the dead was banned in the Old Testament and had a very severe punishment, 'A man or a woman who is a medium or a fortune teller must be put to death' (Leviticus 20:27). Many people attend meetings (séances) where they attempt to contact ghosts and believe that they have contacted the dead. Others claim that séances are situations that are faked by people who wish to take advantage of those who are grieving. On some Sky TV channels you can watch mediums pass on messages from the dead.

Reincarnation

Reincarnation is generally considered to be a religious reason for believing in life after death. However, there are those who believe that this is just the moving on of the essence of a person from one body to another and does not involve a God or religion. Evidence from this can be found in experiences of déjà vu (the feeling of familiarity in a new situation) or memories of past lives.

For discussion

What do you think about the evidence of life after death from a non-religious point of view? Do you believe in ghosts, the power of mediums or stories of near-death experiences? What are your reasons for this point of view?

Why some non-religious people do not believe in life after death

Many non-religious people do not believe in life after death in any form. For them:

- If death is the end, how can there be more? If there is more, then it is not the end and therefore not death.
- There is no evidence for an afterlife.
- Religion offers no good reasons to believe in an afterlife.
- Religious beliefs in an afterlife may be harmful.
- Ideas of Heaven and Hell are simply made up.
- Mediums and other people who attempt to prove there is an afterlife are tricking people.
- In an age when science explains the world, we should not believe in things that are unscientific.
- When a person dies their body decays so how can they live again?
- Life after death is simply impossible – we are either alive or dead.

Activities

1 In the film *Ghost*, the way death is presented is similar to that of immortality of the soul, although religious beliefs about death are not mentioned at all in the film. How could the film writers have included these?

2 The medium explains that ghosts are trapped souls who have unfinished business. In this film, the afterlife is a reward or punishment for the actions committed during life. Can this take place without a God?

3 Write a list of other films, TV dramas or storylines in soap operas that explore the issue of life after death. Does the media represent the beliefs of religious people fairly?

4 In your own words, outline why some people do not believe in life after death.

How life after death is covered in a film

In this section you will be asked to consider how an issue arising from matters of life and death has been presented in one form of media – the example of the film *Ghost* is one you could use. You will be asked to describe how the issue was covered, and whether the treatment of the issue was fair to religious beliefs and religious people.

In the film Ghost *no religious reasons are given for life after death, although a lot of religious symbolism is used.*

Summary

- Many non-religious people believe in life after death because of things such as near-death experiences, ghosts and contacting the dead.
- Others reject life after death as being impossible.

2.4 The nature of abortion, including current legislation

36

Learning outcomes

By the end of this lesson you should be able to:

- give a personal response to the questions 'When does life begin?' and 'Is it ever right to kill?' with reasons for that point of view
- explain how the answers to these two questions affect a person's attitude towards abortion
- outline the current law on abortion in the United Kingdom
- explain why abortion is a controversial issue
- give reasons for and against abortion.

edexcel ⠿ key terms

Abortion – The removal of a foetus from the womb before it can survive.

The decision as to whether **abortion** is right or wrong is based on the answers to the two key questions on the previous pages. Abortion is controversial because there are many different opinions about when life begins and if it is ever right to kill.

When does life begin?

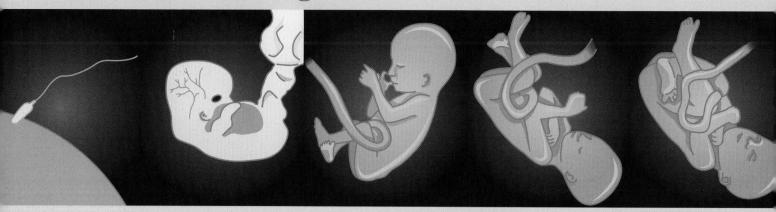

At fertilisation, the genetic make-up and the sex of the embryo are determined.

At conception, the sperm and ovum meet and an embryo comes into existence.

Week 3: organs have begun to develop; there is a nervous system and blood vessels.

Week 4: the eyes and ears are visible; the heart begins to pump and teeth begin to form.

Week 5: facial features are recognisable.

Week 6: movement begins.

Week 7: leg and arm movements occur; fingers can be seen; head movements begin.

Week 8: eyelids are closing, breathing movements are evident, the embryo can be startled. The embryo becomes known as a foetus.

Week 9: hair begins to grow and the foetus can yawn.

Week 10: fingernails develop and the sucking reflex begins.

Week 12: the physical body is complete. It can swallow, close its hand and its sexual organs can be identified.

Week 16: it is about this time that a woman first feels movement.

Week 22: the foetus shows evidence of hearing things outside the womb. A foetus born at this time will attempt to breathe.

Activities

1 Imagine that you have been given the power to create a the law on abortion. In the middle of a large piece of paper write down what laws and/or guidelines you would introduce.

2 In pairs, discuss the consequences that might occur if this was enforced in the UK today.

Make a note of these consequences around your work. Do your laws need changing? Why?

For discussion

Once we have established that something is alive, when would it be acceptable to end that life? Is it acceptable to take something away that you cannot replace?

Activities

3 Look at the images and information on these pages and decide when you think life begins. Your answer to this question will help you to make decisions about the next few issues. Make a note of your decision. What were your reasons for choosing this point?

4 Discuss your answer with different members of the class. How can you decide who is right and who is wrong?

5 At what stage did the development of this human begin to have the potential to become fully a human being? What determines when someone is 'alive'? What is life?

6 When is life more important? When it is an embryo? When it is a foetus? When it is a baby? A teenager? An adult? An old person?

Is it ever right to kill?

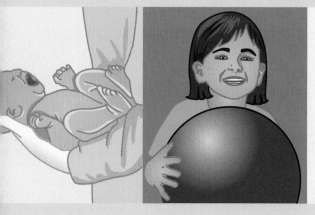

Week 26: lungs are capable of breathing air; the nervous system begins to regulate the body's temperature.

The development now continues with growth and an increase in weight.

38–40 weeks: the foetus leaves the womb and breathes by itself. At this point it becomes known as a baby.

0–1 year: the baby requires feeding, physical contact and support in getting around. It would not survive without outside assistance.

5 years: the child is moving independently, and still needs help from adults.

15 years: the young person is increasingly independent, but still needs adults to advise regularly on keeping safe and appropriate human behaviour.

16–40 years: the human being can reproduce and create new human life.

40–60 years: the human being begins to slow down, the body begins to show signs of wear and often needs medical assistance.

60+: the ageing human being is increasingly dependent on younger humans and medical care for survival.

What does UK law say?

The current law on abortion is based on the 1967 Abortion Act and the Human Fertilisation and Embryology Act of 1990. Before 1967, abortion was illegal in the UK.

The current law on abortion states that an abortion can take place up to the 24th week of pregnancy, if two doctors agree that:

- continuing the pregnancy would pose a risk to the physical or mental health of the woman
- the physical or mental health of the woman's existing children would suffer if a new baby was born
- if the child were born it would be seriously mentally or physically handicapped.

Abortion is allowed after 24 weeks if there is:

- a risk to the woman's life
- evidence that the baby will be severely handicapped
- risk of serious physical and mental injury to the woman.

Abortion must be carried out by a doctor in government-approved NHS or private hospital or clinic.

Activities

7 Read the current law on abortion carefully. How does it compare with the law you wrote? What are your thoughts about the UK law? Explain your answer.

8 Can you think of any circumstances where a women could not have an abortion before 24 weeks?

9 Should doctors have the right to refuse to carry out an abortion?

For discussion

Whose life is more important, the foetus or the mother's? Give reasons for your opinion.

Arguments for and against abortion

People who believe that the mother should be able to choose whether to have an abortion are called 'pro-choice'. People who believe that the child has a right to life are called 'pro-life'. Let's look at what these people believe in more detail.

I think that it is the best option, the lesser of two evils, in some situations. For example, if the child will be born with a severe disability or terminal illness, or if the mother's life is at risk if the pregnancy continues. It is the best option given the choices

I think that it is the woman's right to choose what happens to her own body. No one has the right to make you carry a foetus for 40 weeks.

I think in the case of rape the child will be unwanted and might cause both the mother and the child itself long-term mental problems.

Susan

The mother might not be able to bring up a child for financial or emotional reasons. For example, a girl under the age of 16 may not be ready to be a mother. In these cases it would be better to end the pregnancy.

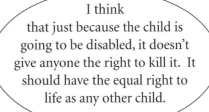

Callum

I believe that life is special and should not be taken at any cost. I believe life begins at conception when the embryo has the potential of becoming a human being.

I think that just because the child is going to be disabled, it doesn't give anyone the right to kill it. It should have the equal right to life as any other child.

I think that the unborn child should have the same human rights as any other human being.

There are always loving parents waiting to adopt who could give the child a loving home at the end of the pregnancy.

ResultsPlus
Exam question report

Explain why people argue about abortion. (8 marks)
June 2007

How students answered

Most of the candidates who scored poorly on this question outlined Christian views on abortion – that is not what the question required.

Many candidates could explain a few of the reasons why abortion is controversial but did not go into enough detail or explain the opposing view. Some did not include the point of view of Christians.

Many candidates scored well on this question because they explained the controversy about abortion giving specific examples (e.g. When does life begin?) and explaining how different people, including Christians, respond to these issues.

Activities

10 Read Susan's arguments for abortion and Callum's arguments against.

- What do you think about Callum's arguments for pro-life?
- What do you think about Susan's arguments for pro-choice?
- Draw yourself in the middle of a page and put your own speech bubbles around showing what you think about abortion and explaining why.

Summary

- People have different opinions about when human life begins and this affects their attitudes to abortion.
- Current UK law allows abortion in certain circumstances.
- There are various different 'pro-life' arguments against abortion and 'pro-choice' arguments for abortion.

2.5 Christian attitudes to abortion

Learning outcomes

By the end of this lesson, you should be able to:

- give a definition of the sanctity of life
- outline the Christian beliefs about abortion and explain why they hold them
- explain why there are different attitudes to abortion within Christianity.

edexcel ::: key terms

Sanctity of life – The belief that life is holy and belongs to God.

The sanctity of life

Christians believe in the **sanctity of life**, or that life is gift from God, is holy and belongs to God. They believe that human beings are made in the image of God and are responsible for God's creation, 'So God created man in his own image. In the image of God he created him: male and female, he created them' (Genesis 1:27). God was involved in the creation of each individual person, 'You knit me together in my mother's womb' (Psalm 139:13).

Conjoined twins born in Guatemala, June 2006.

Activities

1   Consider the Christian point of view that life is holy. What three questions would you ask a Christian about this teaching?

2   How can life be holy and special when it is not perfect – for example, the birth of conjoined twins or when someone has a genetic condition?

3   Would there be as many abortions if you could see the developing foetus while it is in the mother? Give your reasons.

Why there are different attitudes to abortion in Christianity

Christians would argue that life begins at conception and that all human life is sacred. One of the Ten Commandments in the Bible says 'You should not kill', therefore, the majority of Christians believe abortion is wrong. However, within Christianity, there are different opinions about abortion.

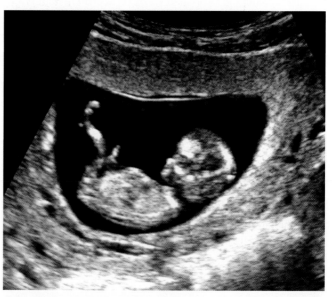

A foetus developing within the womb.

40

Attitudes towards abortion

Who	Believes what	Why
Most Roman Catholics and evangelical Christians	Are against abortion	• They believe life begins at conception and is created in the image of God. • The foetus is alive and murder is wrong according to the Bible. • Life is a gift from God and only God can take it away. • God has a plan for every life and we should not interfere with that plan. • Some foetuses are aborted because they are not going to be perfect human beings. There appears to be a pre-birth test for unborn babies to pass before they are allowed to be born. • The Catechism (official teachings) of the Roman Catholic Church says 'Abortion is a horrible crime… the law must provide appropriate sanctions for every deliberate violation of the child's rights'. • In special cases there is 'The doctrine of double effect'. This is the idea that deciding to perform one operation might trigger another. For example, if a woman needs treatment for cancer and that treatment would kill her unborn child, then this would be allowed. It is not abortion because the doctor was curing the cancer not aborting the foetus.
The Church of England	Generally opposes abortion but allows it in some cases	• If it is the most loving thing to do, for example in cases of rape or incest, or when the mother's life is at risk. Jesus told Christians to love their neighbour as themselves. They accept the idea that sometimes it can be the 'lesser of two evils'. • The Church of England, according to the General Synod (the governing body of the Church of England), strongly opposes abortion with a recognition that there can be in some extreme circumstances a need for it to take place, when no alternative way can be found.
Other more liberal Christians	Oppose abortion but consider it the lesser of two evils	• Jesus acted with love and compassion and so Christians must do the same. • God gave us free will and people must make the right choices for themselves. • Modern technology allows the early detection of conditions and diseases that will cause suffering later. These tests and abortions should be accepted to prevent suffering. • Sometimes it is right to kill, especially in self-defence or to save the mother's life. • They believe that life begins later in the pregnancy or at birth, not at conception.

For discussion

• Does the situation a person finds themselves in at any given time mean they have the right to kill?

• What is the difference between killing a foetus at 24 weeks and a baby at four weeks after birth? Refer back to the photograph of the developing foetus.

Activities

4 Give a presentation to your class about your view on abortion and how it differs or agrees with that of Christians.

Summary

• The majority of Christians believe that abortion is wrong.

• Some Christians accept that, in certain circumstances, it is the lesser of two evils.

2.6 The nature of euthanasia

Learning outcomes

By the end of this lesson, you should be able to:

- outline the current law on euthanasia in the United Kingdom
- explain why euthanasia is a controversial issue
- give reasons for and against euthanasia.

edexcel ⠿ key terms

Assisted suicide – Providing a seriously ill person with the means to commit suicide.

Euthanasia – The painless killing of someone dying from a painful disease.

Non-voluntary euthanasia – Ending someone's life painlessly when they are unable to ask, but you have good reason for thinking they would want you to do so – e.g. switching off a life-support machine.

Voluntary euthanasia – Ending life painlessly when someone in great pain asks for death.

Euthanasia and the law

In the UK all forms of **euthanasia** are against the law. Anyone assisting euthanasia could be accused of murder, although this can be reduced to manslaughter in some cases. The fact that a patient wants to die is not a defence in the UK. There have been several cases where permission has been given to allow passive euthanasia.

Euthanasia: a good death.

Voluntary euthanasia: where a patient who is dying in pain requests a doctor to end their life gently.

Non-voluntary euthanasia: is carried out where the patient is unable to ask for it but the people around think this is what the patient would have wanted.

Active euthanasia: is carried out by a doctor on purpose, such as the giving of a lethal injection.

Passive euthanasia: is when medical treatment or a life-support machine is withdrawn, or when treatment is refused and the person is allowed to die.

A person's right to choose

Many people are in favour of euthanasia because:

- It allows the patient to die a gentle, pain-free death and to exercise their right to die as they choose.
- The patient dies with dignity, rather than slowly getting worse, mentally and physically.
- Euthanasia saves medical costs.
- Medics can focus their attention on patients who have a chance of recovery.
- It relieves the family of emotional and financial burdens.

For discussion

Do you think people should be allowed to choose how and when they die? Why?

People who argue against euthanasia consider it a 'slippery slope'. This means that if voluntary euthanasia were legalised for the terminally ill who were in severe pain, then it would start to happen in other circumstances too. If this happened, then there would be less medical research that would diminish the value of life even more and put pressure on the sick and dying to choose euthanasia rather than to seek a cure.

In 1993, the House of Lords rejected a proposal to legalise euthanasia, saying 'It would be next to impossible to ensure that all acts of euthanasia were truly voluntary'.

ResultsPlus
Watch out!

Some candidates get confused between abortion and euthanasia – make sure that you know the definition of both words.

Activities

1   In *Holby City* there was a long-running storyline of a woman (Gina Hope) who wanted to choose when she died. She was dying a slow and painful death. Eventually, Gina convinced a friend to take her to an **assisted suicide** clinic in Switzerland, where she died peacefully in her husband's arms. For further information, go to www.heinemann. co.uk/hotlinks (express code 4202P) and click on the appropriate link.

    Write a list of other films, TV dramas or storylines in soap operas that have explored the issue of euthanasia. Do you think the media represents the beliefs of religious people fairly?

Activities

2   Explain why some people think the law on euthanasia in the UK should be changed. What do you think about this? Give reasons for your answer.

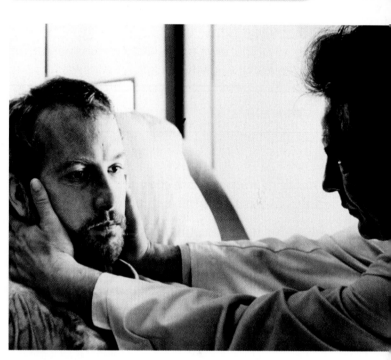

In the film Whose Life is it Anyway? *Ken Harrison is an artist who makes sculptures. One day he was involved in a car accident, and is paralysed from his neck. All he can do is talk and he wants to die. In hospital he makes friends with some of the staff and they support him when he goes to court to be allowed to die. He argues a strong case for the right to die.*

Summary

- Euthanasia means helping people to die to save them from pain.
- Euthanasia is currently illegal in the UK.
- There are many arguments for and against euthanasia.

2.7 Christian attitudes to euthanasia

Learning outcomes

By the end of this lesson, you should be able to:

- outline different Christian attitudes to euthanasia
- explain why Christians have these different views
- give your own opinions on these different views with reasons why you think this.

edexcel ⠿ key terms

Quality of life – The idea that life must have some benefits for it to be worth living.

Euthanasia and the sanctity of life

Most Christians object to euthanasia because it goes against the principle of the sanctity of life.

Christians who are more accepting of the possibility of euthanasia may use the argument that God intends that humans should have a good **quality of life.** This means that they should be able to do the things that are meaningful to them and make them feel good about life.

Attitudes towards euthanasia

Who	What	Why
Most Christians	It is wrong	• It is taking away the life of a human being that is always murder. • God created human beings in his image so only God has the power to take life away. • Even if a sick person says they want to die, no one has the authority to take their life away. • Life is so valuable it should be valued even when someone is in great pain. • Terminally ill patients can still worship God and show other people God's love. • Euthanasia could be used for evil purposes. • Doctors or relatives may make the choice without consulting the patient. • No one should be able to make a judgement about the value of another person's life. • No person should value themselves as so worthless it would be better to die. • The Catechism of the Roman Catholic Church states 'An act or omission that causes death in order to eliminate suffering constitutes a murder greatly contrary to the dignity of the human person and to the respect due to the living God, his Creator'.
Some Christians	Would allow the giving of powerful pain-killing drugs (that will shorten life)	• The quality of life would be improved.
Other Christians	Allow the turning off of a life-support machine	• The life has already ended.

Dianne Pretty with her husband.

Preparation for death

Many Christians believe that death itself is a spiritual time because the dying person is getting closer to God and preparing for the afterlife. It would therefore be wrong to interfere with this process. They work to provide hospice care for these patients. The Christian Hospice Movement states that they are able to control pain in patients with terminal cancer. They believe that euthanasia is unnecessary, wrong and an admission of defeat.

Activities

5 Refer back to the answer you gave to the questions 'When does life begin?' and 'Is it ever right to kill?'. Has your opinion changed? Why?

Summary

- Most Christians are strongly opposed to euthanasia on the grounds that life is a gift from God and no one has the right to take it away.
- Rather than encourage people to see euthanasia as an option, Christians should work to help people who are dying by offering effective pain relief and helping them to prepare for death.

Dianne Pretty was terminally ill and wanted her husband to help her to die. He agreed, but the European Court of Human Rights said that he was not allowed to help her. The fight for the right to die and the arguments used are available on the Internet.

For most Christians, the principle of the sanctity of life outweighs this and everyone, no matter how ill or disabled, has a precious life to live. They believe that all people should be valued equally, whatever their physical or mental condition, whether they are old, or not even conscious. All people should therefore be treated with dignity. Some people claim that euthanasia is like putting an animal down who is suffering.

Activities

1 Research the story of Dianne Pretty on the Internet.
2 Imagine you are in the European Court. What arguments would Dianne Pretty have put forward and how would the judge have responded?
3 What would Christians say to her?
4 What would you say to her?

2.8 The causes of world poverty

> ### Learning outcome
> By the end of this lesson, you should be able to:
> - explain the causes of world poverty.

Standard of living

Most people would accept that we live in a developed country. We have the resources we need to have a long life and a good standard of living – a good quality of life. Those countries that do not have the resources to provide what is needed for a long life and a good standard of living are called Less Economically Developed Countries (LEDCs). Some countries are in between and are considered to be 'developing' countries.

What causes world poverty?

Many things contribute to world poverty. However, the causes may differ for each country and some causes contribute to others.

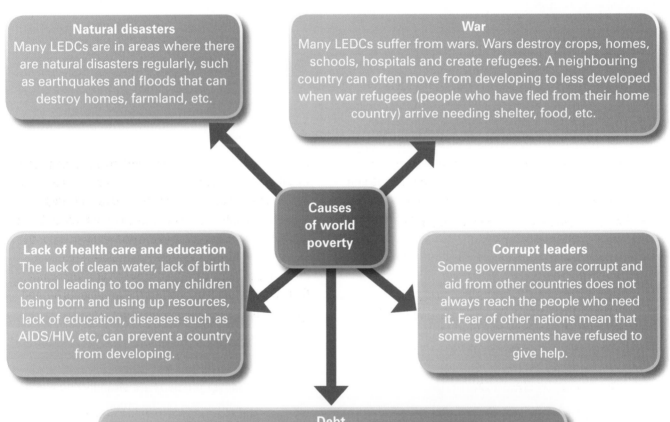

Natural disasters
Many LEDCs are in areas where there are natural disasters regularly, such as earthquakes and floods that can destroy homes, farmland, etc.

War
Many LEDCs suffer from wars. Wars destroy crops, homes, schools, hospitals and create refugees. A neighbouring country can often move from developing to less developed when war refugees (people who have fled from their home country) arrive needing shelter, food, etc.

Causes of world poverty

Lack of health care and education
The lack of clean water, lack of birth control leading to too many children being born and using up resources, lack of education, diseases such as AIDS/HIV, etc, can prevent a country from developing.

Corrupt leaders
Some governments are corrupt and aid from other countries does not always reach the people who need it. Fear of other nations mean that some governments have refused to give help.

Debt
All LEDCs suffer from debt. They have to borrow money from banks in developed countries and pay large amounts of interest to the bank that they could have spent on development. Many LEDCs try to get money from abroad by growing and selling crops but rich countries pay their farmers grants (subsidies) to grow crops and put high taxes on the crops from LEDCs so their goods are expensive. Then they export the crops their farmers have grown at prices that are lower than the LEDCs can grow them for.

Child famine victim in Sudan.

For discussion

- What questions does the photograph above raise about matters of life and death? What feelings and emotions do you have when you see this? Why?
- How can someone end up in this situation?

Cash crops

Many poor countries try to solve their poverty by growing cash crops (for example, cotton, tea, coffee, etc.) to sell to the more economically developed countries, but this uses land that might have grown food, and can cause starvation.

Activities

1 Outline the causes of world poverty.
2 How many of these causes are man-made problems?
3 Which of the causes could be helped by charities?

Think about it

If you used the argument for abortion and euthanasia that it could be justified on the grounds of the person not having a good quality of life, where does this leave the people in less developed countries, or those living in poverty in Britain? Hitler believed that he was solving a problem with his 'euthanasia programme' that killed millions of people. How do you feel about that? Do you need to consider the arguments for and against abortion and euthanasia again?

Summary

- The world is full of people who live in poverty.
- Many of the causes of poverty are linked to each other.

2.9 Why Christians work to end world poverty

Learning outcomes

By the end of this lesson you should be able to:

- describe the work of one Christian agency that is trying to end world poverty
- explain why Christians work to try to end world poverty.

Why Christians work to end world poverty

Christians use the teachings of Jesus to direct them in how they should respond to poverty.

Most Christians believe that they should help the poor because of the teachings from the Bible.

Jesus taught that his followers should have compassion towards the poor. '*Love your neighbour as you love yourself*' (Luke 10:27). When he was asked to explain this he told the story of the Good Samaritan (Luke 10: 25–37).

The Bible also promotes justice – the principle that everyone has the right to be treated fairly. God created everyone equal, it is wrong therefore to ignore the needs of others. It is a duty to care for others less fortunate.

Christians are also taught about stewardship. In terms of poverty this means that they should use their wealth wisely to help others. Christians are encouraged to give to charities and tithe their income.

Giving does not always have to be money. Christians also believe that it is equally as valuable to give time to help the poor. Many Christians give their time or whole lives to support the poor – for example, Mother Teresa. She spent her whole life helping the poor, but she never had any money to donate.

Jesus looked at him and loved him. 'One thing you lack', he said, 'Go sell everything you have and give to the poor, and you will have treasure in Heaven. Then come, follow me.' Then the man's face fell. He went away sad because he had great wealth. Jesus looked round and said to his disciples, 'How hard it is for the rich to enter the kingdom of God.'
Mark 10:21–23

'What good is it, my brothers, if a man claims to have faith but has no deeds? Can his faith save him? Suppose a brother or sister is without clothes and daily food. If one of you says to him, 'Go, I wish you well; keep warm and well fed,' but does nothing about his physical needs, what good is it? In the same way faith by itself, if it is not accompanied by action is dead.'
James 2:14–17

'I was hungry and you fed me, thirsty and you gave me a drink; I was a stranger and you received me into your homes, I was naked and you clothed me; I was sick and you took care of me, I was in prison and you visited me,' he told his followers. They were surprised by this answer because they had never seen Jesus in such a state but he explained, 'I tell you, whenever you did this for one of the least important of these brothers of mine, you did it for me.'
Matthew 25:35–40

For discussion

After reading these quotes from the Bible, how would you expect a Christian to respond to the problem of poverty? Why would you expect this?

Many Christian charities provide essential supplies and workers to help in less economically developed parts of the world and in times of emergency.

Christian organisations

Some Christians have set up organisations and charities that work to relieve world poverty. Christian Aid and CAFOD (the Catholic Fund for Overseas Development) are examples of organisations that work around the world to help people in need.

Activities

1 As part of your study, you will need to research one of these agencies and find out about the work they do and how it relates to their Christian beliefs. Both organisations have websites and information that they will share with you.

Use the Christian Aid website to research the work done by Christian Aid and how it relates to their Christian beliefs. Go to www.heinemann.co.uk/hotlinks (express code 4202P) and click on the appropriate link.

Use this CAFOD website to research the work done by CAFOD and how it relates to their Christian beliefs. Go to www.heinemann.co.uk/hotlinks (express code 4202P) and click on the appropriate link.

49

For discussion

Is it easier to give money or time?

Trocaire is a charity based in Ireland. It was set up to show the Irish Churches' concern for those who are suffering in the world and for those who are poor and oppressed.

Trocaire supports development work in 39 countries in Africa, Asia, Latin America and the Middle East.

The work they do aims to:

- build a reliable way of life and help people cope with climate change
- respond to emergencies and disasters
- tackle injustice and defend human rights
- address the HIV and AIDS crisis
- support gender equality.

Activities

2 After your research in Activity 1, create a leaflet or poster to advertise the work of the agency of your choice. You should include:

- the types of work they carry out
- the reasons for this work (including biblical teachings)
- reasons why Christians should support this charity.

Summary

- Christians follow the example of Jesus in helping to relieve poverty in the world.
- This has led to the setting up of Christian organisations such as CAFOD and Christian Aid that work throughout the world.

2.10 Matters of life and death in the media

Learning outcomes

By the end of this lesson, you should be able to:

- explain how different forms of media tackle matters of life and death
- describe examples of storylines in newspapers, films or national press that cover a matter raised in this section
- give evidence from the media to explain whether the coverage was fair or unfair to religious people
- give your opinion on how these issues were covered and whether the media should be allowed to criticise religious beliefs.

Types of media

There are several forms of media that present issues of life and death to the public.

During this section, programmes on the TV that have covered the issues of death, life after death, abortion, euthanasia and poverty have been discussed. You may study more with your teacher, as these are all good examples to use in your answers to the GCSE questions. The more evidence you have the better.

Activities

1 Look at this week's newspapers. How many stories are about matters of life and death?

2 In the same way, watch the news on TV. Explain how it deals with issues of life and death.

3 Are there any differences between the newspaper and TV? Why do you think this is so?

Soap operas

Events in soap operas regularly include issues about family and relationships as well as issues such as abortion, euthanasia, and how people cope with illness and death. A single storyline will not tend to dominate a drama. Instead, several stories will be woven together over an unlimited number of episodes. The focus is on how events affect familiar characters so that the viewers may consider how they themselves would respond. If a particularly emotional issue has been addressed by a soap, then a helpline telephone number is often given at the end, so that viewers who have been affected by this issue may get support or extra information.

Activities

4 Choose one type of media and describe a storyline that covers death, abortion, euthanasia or poverty. Explain how the issue was dealt with. Present this work as a spider diagram, putting the issue in the middle and adding around it the different opinions.

5 Were all the sides of the argument presented? Was a religious response to the issue included? If not, why do you think this was missed out? If it was covered, do you think it was a fair portrayal of religious people's beliefs?

Newspapers

Newspapers take their responsibility to communicate news about matters of life and death very seriously. As there are so many different newspapers, with different styles and emphases, you will be able to look at how an ethical issue is covered from several angles. Each newspaper will usually have a relatively predictable response, depending on its target readership. While some newspapers are more open about offering an opinion, others will appear to be unbiased, although contributions from medical, legal, or academic experts will present the case from differing perspectives.

The scene shortly after a terrorist bombing.

For discussion

- Should newspapers and TV show pictures such as these, or should they be censored first? Give your reasons.

- What considerations might need to be taken before a newspaper prints a story or picture concerning a tragic death? Why?

- Newspapers and TV news reports sometimes challenge the beliefs of religious people about issues – for example, abortion and euthanasia. It is not always a direct criticism; it may be implied in the way the story is reported.

- Do you think the media should be allowed to criticise religious beliefs?

Films and documentaries

A surprising number of films are made that tackle matters of life and death. In most cases, the moral theme of a film is presented alongside the more usual themes of popular film (such as romance, family dramas, adventures or fantasy) because most films are designed to entertain as well as inform. If the director simply wanted to educate the audience about an issue of life or death, then they would produce a documentary rather than a feature film. There are many useful documentaries on TV that cover life and death issues (for example, rare illnesses or disabilities, or the cases of individuals who have to make difficult choices) that often may not reach a wide public audience. Even in feature films, the director may choose to focus the whole film on a moral issue.

For discussion

- Do films and documentaries show life and death in greater detail than newspapers and TV?

- Should a director be impartial, or should he or she present opinions on an issue for us to discuss and consider?

Activities

6 Write a short review of a film you have seen that dealt with matters of life and death. Give your opinion on how well or how badly the subject was treated and whether it was accurate and fair.

Summary

- A wide range of media can be used to present matters of life and death to a wide audience.

- Newspapers and TV news, soap opera, documentaries and films all take some responsibility for presenting issues to the public.

- Each form of media has different intentions and interests; some may reflect the opinions of the programme makers or editors while others are more impartial.

examzone

Know Zone
Matters of life and death

Quick quiz

1   What is meant by non-voluntary euthanasia?

2   Give two examples of the paranormal.

3   Outline the UK law on abortion.

4   Why do some non-religious people believe in life after death?

5   Outline Christian beliefs in life after death.

6   What is meant by the sanctity of life.

7   Outline the causes of world poverty

8   Do you think abortion should be allowed? Give reasons for your answer.

9   Why should Christians help to relieve world poverty?

10 Name one Christian organisation that works to relieve world poverty.

Plenary activity

Find out about one person who either currently, or in recent history, has played a significant role in shaping the public's opinion on matters of life and death. For example, you could research into the life of Dianne Pretty who carried out important work campaigning for the right for chronically sick patients to be helped to end their life. Other figures may be Joni Earekson Tada, the Christian quadriplegic, or Terry Schiavo, whose case was so controversial.

Prepare a presentation on this person for the rest of the class, ensuring that you don't just give facts about them, but try to assess how important their case was for publicising such matters and whether you think they had any significant impact on developments in attitudes towards matters of life and death.

Find out more

To find out about Christian research, education and political lobbying about life and death issues, go to www.heinemann.co.uk/hotlinks (express code 4202P) and click on the appropriate link.

Investigate a hospice that promotes care for the dying in your local area.

The British Pregnancy Advisory Service can be used to research information on abortion. Go to www.heinemann.co.uk/hotlinks (express code 4202P) and click on the appropriate link.

Student tips

When I studied my GCSE in Religious Studies I made the mistake of thinking that all Christians felt the same about issues such as abortion or euthanasia. It was a surprise to me to find out that as their views are varied as those of non-believers. You can never say 'all Christians believe...' and be absolutely right. The most you can say is that 'some Christians... ' or 'many Christians believe... '

Self-evaluation checklist

Look at the following table. How would you rate your understanding of this topic? Use the following code to judge your status:

Green – I understand this fully.
Orange – I am confident I can answer most questions on this.
Red – I need to do a lot more work on this topic.

Now answer the following questions:

- Do you hold an opinion on this topic and could you give reasons for that opinion if asked?
- Can you give the opinion of someone who disagrees with you and give reasons why they hold this opinion?

Content covered	My understanding is red/orange/green	Can I give my opinion?	Can I give an alternative opinion?
Why Christians believe in life after death and how their beliefs about life after death affect their lives.			
Non-religious reasons for believing in life after death (near-death experiences, ghosts, mediums, evidence of reincarnation).			
Why some people do not believe in life after death.			
The nature of abortion, including current British legislation.			
The arguments for and against abortion.			
Different Christian attitudes to abortion and the reasons for them.			
The nature of euthanasia including current British legislation.			
Arguments for and against euthanasia.			
Different Christian attitudes to euthanasia and the reasons for them.			
The causes of world poverty.			
How and why one Christian agency is trying the end world poverty.			
How the media presents matters of life and death.			

Introduction

In the exam you will see a choice of two questions on this section. Each question will include four tasks that test your knowledge, understanding and evaluation of the material covered. A 2-mark question will ask you to define a term; a 4-mark question will ask your opinion on a point of view; an 8-mark question will ask you to explain a particular belief or idea; a 6-mark question will ask for your opinion on a point of view and ask you to consider an alternative point of view.

Give a glossary definition. You do not need to write any more – often this can be done in one sentence.

Mini exam paper

(a) What is **non-voluntary euthanasia**? (2 marks)

(b) Do you agree with euthanasia?
Give **two** reasons for your point of view. (4 marks)

(c) Explain why some Christians do not agree with abortion. (8 marks)

(d) 'Your soul will never die.'
In your answer you should refer to Christianity.

(i) Do you agree? Give reasons for your opinion. (3 marks)

(ii) Give reasons why some people may disagree with you. (3 marks)

Give your opinion, but note that marks are only awarded for the reasons you have for thinking that opinion is correct. Each reason needs to be explained to gain the marks available.

The 'explain why' questions are asking for you to give reasons. In this case the best way would be to give four reasons and explain them fully. It is possible to get to the highest level with two reasons but you must develop them fully. Once the examiner has awarded the level for your answer, they will look at the quality of your spelling and punctuation and will use this to decide if you gain 7 or 8 marks. Be aware on the C questions to use formal English and check your spellings etc.

The (d) question is split into two parts – answer each part separately. You must refer to the statement and Christian beliefs during this whole question. It may be worth considering whether Christians would agree or disagree with this statement and use their reasons in (ii) and then provide the alternative point of view as your own.

(i) You must give one very well-explained reason for your opinion or three simple reasons to gain full marks.

(ii) You must now show you understand the reasons that someone might disagree with you.

Mark scheme

(a) You will earn **2 marks** for a correct answer, and **1 mark** for a partially correct answer.

(b) To earn up to the full **4 marks** you need to give two reasons (as asked) and to develop them fully. Two brief reasons will earn **2 marks** and one reason without development will earn **1 mark**.

(c) You can earn **7–8 marks** by giving up to four reasons, but the fewer reasons you give, the more you must develop them. You are being assessed on your use of language so you also need to take care to express your understanding in a clear style of English, and make some use of specialist vocabulary.

(d) To go beyond **3 marks** for the whole of this question you must refer to Christianity. The more you are able to develop your reasons, the more marks you will earn. Three simple reasons can earn you the same mark as one fully developed reason.

ResultsPlus
Maximise your marks

(c) Explain why some Christians do not agree with abortion. (8 marks)

Student answer	Examiner comments	Improved student answer
Christians have different views on abortion but all believe that it is wrong because it violates the sanctity of life. Some Christians believe that life is so valuable that abortion can never happen, while other Christians believe that there are times when the woman has a right to choose to have an abortion, for example, if she has been raped, or if she will suffer physically or mentally from the pregnancy or having the child.	The question asks why some Christians disagree with abortion so there is no reason to mention those who do. Because the question asks 'why', the answer should give two reasons developed or four reasons; these should be identifiable by the word 'because'.	Some Christians do not agree with abortion because they believe that life begins at conception and one of the Ten Commandments is 'You shall not murder'. Therefore, if the foetus is alive, it is wrong to kill it. Christians also believe that life is a gift from God and only he has the right to take it. Therefore, taking the life of an unborn child is murder, and as God has a plan for every life, aborting the unborn child interferes with this plan.
Most Christians would say that they didn't agree with abortion because it is never a good thing, but some would say this means that abortions should never happen, while others would say that, although it is wrong, it may sometimes be the lesser of two evils.	In this answer the student mentions the sanctity of life, and develops this by saying that life is valuable, so abortion can never happen. This would gain 4 marks. The student then goes on to give reasons why some Christians allow abortion, but this does not add anything to the answer.	In the teachings of the Roman Catholic Church it says 'abortion is a horrible crime' and therefore most Catholics would believe this too.

Marriage and the family

Introduction

In this section you will learn about the attitudes and beliefs Christians have towards sex outside marriage, marriage, and divorce. You will consider changing attitudes to these topics. You will learn about Christian attitudes to contraception and homosexuality. You will evaluate the alternative points of view on these issues and come to a personal conclusion with reasons to support it.

Learning outcomes for this section

By the end of this section you will be able to:

- give definitions of the key terms and use them in answers to GCSE questions
- outline the changes in attitudes in the UK to sex outside of marriage, marriage, divorce, family life and homosexuality, and give reasons for this
- describe different Christian attitudes to sex outside of marriage, explain why there are different attitudes and express your own point of view with reasons
- explain the purpose of marriage in Christianity and how this is shown through the marriage ceremony
- describe different Christian attitudes to homosexuality, explain why there are different attitudes and express your own point of view with reasons
- outline the Christian teachings on family life and its importance
- describe how Christian Churches help with the upbringing of children and explain how this helps keep the family together
- outline different methods of contraception and explain why they are used
- evaluate, with examples, how these issues have been covered on the media.

edexcel ::: key terms

adultery	contraception	nuclear family	promiscuity
civil partnership	faithfulness	pre-marital sex	re-constituted family
cohabitation	homosexuality	procreation	re-marriage

57

1 List as many variations of 'family' as you can.
2 Look at the photos on this page. Which is the odd one out? Give reasons for your answer. Compare your thoughts with the person sitting beside you.
3 Thinking about your own future, do you want to get married? What are you hoping for when you get married: children, a life-long arrangement?
4 Do you think attitudes to marriage and the family have changed? Give reasons for your answer. Do young people today still hope to have the happy-ever-after life of Cinderella? Why or why not?
5 Consider how the media used to present the family. Look, for example, at Walt Disney's *Cinderella* made in 1950. How have things changed? Do you think the media has played a part in the changing attitudes towards sex, marriage, divorce and families?

Fascinating fact

Did you know that, in 2007, the provisional divorce rate in England and Wales fell to 11.9 divorcing people per 1000 married population compared with the 2006 figure of 12.2? The divorce rate was at its lowest level since 1981. At the same time, fewer people are getting married. This is due to a number of reasons, including a decline in religious belief.

3.1 Changing attitudes to marriage, divorce, family and homosexuality in the UK

58

Learning outcomes

By the end of this lesson, you should be able to:

- describe the changes in attitudes in the UK to marriage, divorce, family life and homosexuality
- explain why there has been a change in attitude
- give your opinion, with reasons, on why things have changed.

edexcel ⣿ key terms

Homosexuality – Sexual attraction to the same sex.

Glossary

Divorce – The legal termination of a marriage.

Marriage – The condition of a man and woman, legally united for the purpose of living together and usually having children.

Reasons for change

In the UK, attitudes towards marriage, divorce, the family and **homosexuality** have changed dramatically in recent years. Changes in attitude towards things like this take time. Generally, society has become more accepting of things that are traditionally considered different and not the 'norm'.

The film Mona Lisa Smile *explored the theme of the role of a woman in the family as things were beginning to change. The film provides many examples of how women were expected to stay at home and how things changing caused problems for some people.*

1   Is change always a good thing?

The reasons for the changes in attitudes towards marriage, divorce, family and homosexuality could be:

- Historical events such as the abolition of slavery and voting rights for women, democracy and the right to free speech. These have allowed other groups to protest for equal rights in society and the success of previous campaigns for equality set a standard of acceptance for all groups of people.
- The view of the world which has become increasingly global. Through technology, media and travel, people come across attitudes and ways of living that are different from their own. They can no longer say this is 'the right way' because, depending where you live, different things are acceptable. Other people may have a different view of the world, values and traditions. This opens people's minds to the possibility of a different response to things.
- The mixture of cultures and ideas that have come to the UK in recent decades, making the country a multi-faith and multi-ethnic society. When people with different traditions and values are living together in one place, a general agreement of what is acceptable is reached and people live together in peace.
- People are more tolerant of the views of others and accepting of differences. Society now tends to celebrate diversity as a positive thing.
- TV has had an impact on the nation. The exploration of issues on programmes such as soap operas, and the presentation of less traditional values as being acceptable, gradually encourages people to accept these situations as the norm. For example, in the 1950s family was presented on TV as an all-white family comprising a stay-at-home mother, a working father and two children. This has now been replaced with working mums, mixed-race families and step-families. The soap opera *EastEnders* has a Muslim family living on the square who face the same issues and problems as the other families and are fully accepted on the square. On *Coronation Street*, a homosexual couple are presented as being completely accepted.
- Greater tolerance and acceptance of people's differences, which have, in turn, reduced the traditional acceptance of Christian teachings and the influence of the Church. The Church has, and still is, deciding on many issues, whether to embrace these changes in attitudes or remain bound by biblical principles.

Activities

2   Write a list of things that have changed for the better and a list of things that have not changed for the better.

In the first episode of *The Vicar of Dibley*, 'The Arrival', a discussion takes place about whether change is good or bad for the village. This is prompted by the arrival of a female vicar. Jim Trott explains to the villagers that there is good change and bad change. He asks the villagers to consider traffic lights and the mess we would be in if there was no change.

For discussion

What do you think about Jim Trott's reflection on change?

Summary

- Attitudes to marriage, divorce, family and homosexuality have changed a great deal in recent years.
- Some people believe this is a good thing as it makes people more free.
- Others believe this is a bad thing and leads to loose-living and a decline in traditional and religious values.

3.2 Christian attitudes to sex outside marriage

Learning outcomes

By the end of this lesson, you should be able to:

- outline biblical teaching on sex outside marriage
- describe the different attitudes to sex outside marriage in Christianity and the reasons for them
- explain why there are different attitudes and the reasons for them
- express, with reasons, your opinion.

edexcel ::: key terms

Adultery – A sexual act between a married person and someone other than their marriage partner.

Cohabitation – Living together without being married.

Faithfulness – Staying with your marriage partner and having sex only with them.

Pre-marital sex – Sex before marriage.

Promiscuity – Having sex with a number of partners without commitment.

The Bible and sexual relationships

The Bible teaches that sex outside marriage is wrong. Sex is an act of love and commitment and should only take place in marriage. This includes having sex before being married (**pre-marital sex**) or having sex with someone when you are already in a relationship with someone else (**adultery**). Christians are taught to avoid having casual sexual relationships (**promiscuity**) and believe married couples should show **faithfulness** to each other.

Activities

1 Write down the quotations from the Bible and say what you think each of them means.

2 Do you agree or disagree with them? Give your reasons.

The Bible says:

> You shall not commit adultery.
> Exodus 20:14

> Do you not know that your body is a temple of the Holy Spirit?
> 1 Corinthians 6:19

> God wants you to be holy and completely free from sexual immorality.
> 1 Thessalonians 4:3 (paraphrased)

> The wife's body does not belong to her alone, but also to her husband. In the same way, the husband's body does not belong to him alone but also to his wife.
> I Corinthians 7:4

> Anyone who looks at a woman lustfully has already committed adultery with her in his heart.
> Matthew 5:28

> The sexual act must take place exclusively within marriage. Outside marriage it always constitutes a grave sin.
> The Catechism of the Catholic Church

Candidates who give the best answers to questions on this section remember that sex outside marriage covers both pre-marital and extra-marital sex. Deal with both in your answers.

Different Christian attitudes

Christians believe that sex outside marriage is wrong because:

- the Bible only allows for sex between marriage partners

- children born outside marriage may have a less stable family life

- promiscuity makes a person vulnerable to sexually transmitted diseases

- loving sexual relations unite a married couple

- adultery breaks the marriage vow of faithfulness.

All Christians think adultery is wrong. A growing number of Christians today do, nevertheless, feel that sex before marriage is acceptable if the couple love each other and they are in a long-term relationship and intend to get married to each other in the future. Indeed, many Christians today think that the teaching of the Bible and the Church on sex before marriage is old-fashioned and out-of-touch with 21st-century values.

Some Christians believe that **cohabitation** that includes sex before marriage should be allowed as a kind of trial marriage. Living with someone helps a couple to discover whether they really will be suited as marriage partners. The Church of England report called 'Something to Celebrate' said that couples who are cohabiting should be acceptable to the Church if this was a step towards marriage.

Activities

3 Consider the storylines in a soap opera for a few weeks. If you removed all the pre-marital and extra-marital sexual relationships, what difference would it make to the quality of the characters' lives?

Activities

4 Do you agree or disagree with the Bible verses on page 60?

Give reasons for your opinion.

Summary

- The Bible teaches that sex should only take place within marriage.
- Different Christians hold different views on this issue.
- Some liberal Christians believe that sex outside marriage is acceptable when it is leading to marriage.

3.3 The purpose of Christian marriage and how this is shown in a wedding ceremony

Learning outcomes

By the end of this lesson, you should be able to:

- outline the purpose of marriage in Christianity
- describe the features of a Christian wedding ceremony and how these symbolise the purpose of marriage.

Christian marriage

Christians believe that marriage is a gift from God. The Roman Catholic Church and the Church of England believe marriage is a sacrament and therefore the bride and groom should be Christian. Other Protestant Churches believe that marriage is very important but not that it is a sacrament and so, in some cases, will allow mixed faith weddings.

> *For this reason a man will leave his father and his mother and be united to his wife, and they will become one flesh.*
> Genesis 2:24

This verse from the Bible suggests that marriage is:

- the mark of the shift in adult responsibility from the parents to the child
- a public occasion, since leaving the parents would have been a cause for celebration with family and friends
- a sexual relationship when two people become one
- between a man and a woman (heterosexual)
- between those two people only (monogamous).

Within Christianity, the purpose of marriage is to:

- have lawful, fulfilling sex
- be faithful to one partner and unite the couple for life
- have children (**procreation**)
- form a secure and safe environment in which to bring up children
- provide love and companionship
- symbolise God's love for the Church.

edexcel ⠿ key terms

Procreation – Making a new life.

Glossary

Sacrament – An outward sign of something holy, usually representing an aspect of God's relationship with human beings.

Activities

1 Do you think that the meaning and purpose of marriage is the same today as it was 100 years ago?

2 If you were to create vows for your own wedding, what would you want to promise and have promised to you? Do you think that you can promise to stay with someone no matter what for the rest of your life?

3 Create a chart as shown in the example below that summarises what marriage is, the purpose of marriage and how this is symbolised in the Christian marriage ceremony.

Marriage

What marriage is	The purpose of marriage	Symbolised in the ceremony by

4 Do you think cohabitation is better than marriage?
   Give two reasons for your answer.

The wedding ceremony

The wedding ceremony then tries to symbolise and celebrate all these beliefs. There are slight variations between the services in different Churches, but the main features are shown below.

The emphasis on God's role in the marriage makes it a spiritual agreement with God as well as a legal agreement.

The congregation pray and ask for God's blessing and support to make the marriage work.

The couple exchange vows that promise a life-long, exclusive commitment to each other.

The verses from the Bible and the words spoken by the vicar emphasise the nature and purpose of marriage for Christians.

The exchange of rings symbolises the unending agreement of marriage.

 ResultsPlus
Build better answers

Explain why marriage is important to Christians.
(8 marks)

■ **Basic, 0–2 mark answers**
These answers will only offer one correct reason.

● **Good, 3–6 mark answers**
These answers will mention some of the different reasons, such as being the best environment in which to raise children and to have lawful sex.

▲ **Excellent, 7–8 mark answers**
The highest marks will be given to those answers that include a variety of opinions and back them up with examples of religious teachings. These answers would include examples such as God's relationship with the Church resembling a marriage.

Summary

- Christians believe that marriage is a gift from God.
- The Christian wedding ceremony symbolises and celebrates the purpose of marriage for Christians.

3.4 Christian attitudes to divorce

Learning outcomes

By the end of this lesson, you should be able to:

- outline the biblical teaching on divorce
- explain why there are different attitudes towards divorce in Christianity
- explain, with reasons, your own opinion about divorce.

Marriage breakdown

A divorce is granted by the courts when a marriage has 'irretrievably broken down' (there is no way that these people can ever stay together). The usual reasons are adultery, unreasonable behaviour or desertion (when one partner leaves the other for a long time).

In the UK about a third of marriages end in divorce and there are about 160,000 divorces each year. People are more inclined to consider getting divorced than they were many years ago. There are a number of reasons for this.

> Divorce is relatively quick and often inexpensive.

> Divorce does not carry the social stigma that it did in the past.

> People are less willing to put up with bad treatment from their partners.

> People are less religious and do not feel bound to their marriage vows.

edexcel ⠿ key terms

Re-marriage – Marrying again after being divorced from a previous marriage.

Glossary

Annulment – A declaration by the Church that a marriage never lawfully existed.

Paul McCartney and Heather Mills had a very expensive and public divorce.

Activities

1 Do you think that when a couple divorces it should be private? Give two reasons for your answer.

2 List other famous divorces. Do you think the high profile that celebrity divorces receive makes divorce more acceptable in people's eyes?

For discussion

Is it too easy to get a divorce? Should it be made more difficult?

For discussion

'Marriage should not have to be for life.' Do you agree? Give two reasons for your view.

Christian attitudes to divorce

Who	What	Why
The Roman Catholic Church	Does not allow divorce	• Jesus said it was wrong, *'Anyone who divorces his wife... and marries another woman commits adultery against her'* (Mark 10:11). • Marriage is a sacrament, a sacred agreement made before God and should not be broken. • The Catechism of the Catholic Church states *'between the baptised, a ratified and consummated marriage cannot be dissolved by any human power or for any other reason than death.'*
	Will allow an annulment of the marriage	If the couple can prove any of the following points: • They did not understand what they were doing. • They were forced into the marriage. • The marriage was not consummated (sexual intercourse did not take place). • One of the partners was not baptised. An annulment can only be granted with the approval of a Catholic Marriage Tribunal.
The Protestant Church	Allows divorce in some circumstances and allows **re-marriage** in church.	• Jesus seemed to allow for divorce in the case of unfaithfulness: *'anyone who divorces his wife, except in the case of unfaithfulness, and marries another commits adultery'* (Matthew 19:9). • Human beings can make mistakes and relationships do break down. • God is always ready to forgive sins. • With God's forgiveness, believers may divorce and find happiness with a different marriage partner. • The Church of England issued a statement on marriage which said that marriage should be seen as a life-long commitment. However, some circumstances arise with the need for divorce to be permissible.
I think…	that	because

Activities

3 Do you think that divorce should be allowed? Complete the chart above with your own opinion and give two reasons for it. Remember that there is a difference between a description of what you think and the reasons for it.

4 What do you think about the Roman Catholic Church's attitude to divorce? Give two reasons for your answer.

5 Should Prince Charles have been allowed to divorce his wife, Princess Diana? Give reasons for your view.

6 What are the main differences between the Catholic and Protestant views of divorce?

7 Which viewpoint would you support and why?

ResultsPlus
Top tip!

The best candidates know which groups of Christians believe what and are careful not to muddle them!

Summary

• The Bible is not always clear about divorce.
• Divorce rates are going up for many different reasons.
• The Catholic Church is opposed to divorce.
• The Protestant Church allows divorce in certain circumstances.

3.5 Christian attitudes to homosexuality

Learning outcomes

By the end of this lesson, you should be able to:

● outline different Christian attitudes to homosexuality

● explain why there are different attitudes to homosexuality in Christianity

● express your own opinion, with reasons.

edexcel ⦂ key terms

Civil partnership – A legal ceremony giving a homosexual couple the same legal rights as a husband and wife.

Attitudes towards homosexuality

Who	What	Why
Many evangelical, conservative Christians	Are strongly opposed to homosexuality and believe homosexuals can be changed by prayer	• *'No man is to have sexual relations with another man; God hates that.'* (Leviticus 18:22) • God created man and woman to be in a marriage relationship together. • Two same-sex partners cannot have a child through natural means. • They believe that homosexuality is not good for society, as it undermines the family. • In the New Testament, Paul writes, *'Neither the sexually immoral… nor homosexual offenders will inherit the Kingdom of God'* (1 Corinthians 6:9–10).
The Roman Catholic Church	Recomends that homosexuals should remain celibate (not have active sexual relationships)	• Based on the biblical teachings, being homosexual is not a sin, but having homosexual sex is. • Roman Catholics believe sex should only take place within marriage. Sex is for procreation and homosexuals cannot marry. Homosexual sex cannot produce children, therefore it is the sexual act that is sinful. • The Catechism of the Roman Catholic Church says that homosexuals 'must be accepted with respect, compassion and sensitivity. Every sign of unjust discrimination in their regard should be avoided.'
The Church of England	Is more sympathetic although divided	• Homosexual partnerships are judged on the strength of the love and commitment of the partners rather than simply rejecting them as wrong; after all, God created us all in his image. • The Church of England accepts that two people might enter into a homosexual relationship with the hope of enjoying companionship and the expression of love similar to that found in marriage.
Other Protestants (such Quakers)	Welcome homosexuals into the Church	• Religion is a spiritual issue not a sexual one. • The Bible needs to be interpreted to suit today's society and Jesus taught that it was love that mattered the most. • Same-sex relationships in the Bible were admired in David and Jonathan, and Ruth and Naomi.

Homosexuality and the media

Attitudes to homosexuality have changed in society. Same-sex couples are often seen on TV, for example in *Coronation Street*.

Sean in Coronation Street.

Sean was introduced to *Coronation Street* viewers in 2003. Sean's life has been a run of ups and downs and challenging relationships. At times the storylines in *Coronation Street* have explored different people's reactions to Sean's sexuality. His best friend Kelly Crabtree got him drunk and tried to seduce him in a bid to change his sexuality and some of the male characters and older residents have found his presence uneasy at times. Overall, the storylines have challenged prejudice and stereotypes. Sean's sexuality is accepted and he is a well-loved character.

Activities

1 Do you think the presentation of homosexual relationships in a soap opera would help to reduce prejudice and promote equality in the world outside of soaps?

2 Do you think homosexuals should be allowed to marry? Give reasons for your view.

3 Outline Christian attitudes to homosexuality.

*In 2005, gay singer Elton John entered into a **civil partnership** with his long-term partner, David Furnish. Civil partnerships were a huge step forward in the recognition of homosexual love and commitment in a relationship.*

Summary

- Most Christians are opposed to homosexuality on the grounds that biblical teachings are against it and that it is not a natural state for human reproductive relationships.

- Although the law is more accepting of homosexual relationships, the Churches are divided, especially in the case of homosexual clergy.

- Some conservative Christian groups preach actively against homosexuality.

- More liberal groups allow that it may be natural and should be accepted to some degree.

3.6 Christian teachings on family life

Learning outcomes

By the end of this lesson, you should be able to:

- outline Christian teachings on family life
- explain why Christians hold certain beliefs about the relationships within the family
- explain how Christian Churches help families
- give your opinion of these beliefs, with reasons.

edexcel ⠿ key terms

Nuclear family – Mother, father and children living as a unit.

Re-constituted family – Where two sets of children (step brothers and step sisters) become one family when their divorced parents marry each other.

Teachings on the family

Christians believe that the family is the basis for a stable society and it is within the family that children learn about God and the Christian faith. In the UK, the people who make up families, and the way families are, has changed over the past 50 years or so from being mostly a **nuclear family** to other variations such as a **re-constituted family**, single-parent families and families with same-sex parents.

The importance of family within Christianity is shown through its inclusion in the Ten Commandments, 'Honour your father and your mother' (Exodus 20:12). The Bible also teaches about the relationship between parents and children, 'Children, obey your parents... Parents, do not exasperate your children; instead, bring them up in the instruction of the Lord' (Ephesians 6:1–4).

Glossary

Extended family – Children, parents and grandparents/aunts/uncles living as a unit or in close proximity.

Single-parent family – One parent living alone with their children as a result of divorce, separation or death, or because the parent is unmarried.

Same-sex family – Two same-sex parents and their children.

Activities

1 Is the traditional family of two heterosexual parents the best form of family? Give two reasons for your answer.

2 Imagine you have been given the responsibility to write a set of guidelines for bringing up a new baby.
   - What would you include?
   - Go beyond the physical needs of the child. How would you provide for its emotional and spiritual needs?
   - How can the values you want to pass on and the nurture of the child best be achieved? Does the child need a family? What purpose does the family serve in the process of nurturing the developing person?

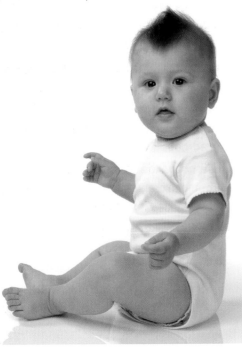

Christians believe that having children is one of the purposes of marriage and that children are a gift from God. Parents have responsibilities towards them to:

- care for them properly
- teach them how to live and to accept authority
- teach them about God
- take their child to be baptised and promise to bring them up in a loving, godly home.

In return, children are expected to respect their parents, and to obey them until they are adults themselves.

How do Christian Churches help families?

Christian Churches try to help parents to raise their children in a stable, Christian environment. The family provides a safe environment for children to learn about relationships. Children learn what is right and wrong, and can make mistakes surrounded by people who will love and support them. When things go wrong, the Church helps by taking the pressure off parents and supporting the family through difficulties, helping the family to stay together. This starts at the beginning of life, when parents bring babies to church for an infant baptism, or dedicate the children to God at a service of dedication and promise to bring them up in a loving Christian home.

As children grow up, they may attend Sunday Schools and youth groups where young people can learn about God in a social environment. Church schools educate children in a Christian environment and many Christian parents choose to send their children to a church or faith school rather than a community school. The extended church family also provides another form of support for the growing young person. The Church provides special support for single parents, sharing and supporting the upbringing of children who have lost a parent through death or divorce.

Activities

3 List the ways in which the Church can help to support Christian families.

4 Explain why family life is so important for Christians.

Churches also hold family services on Sundays and special services at Christmas, Easter and Harvest Festival. They may also help in the running of such organisations as the Scouts and the Brownies. Many churches will have a time in the weekly service that is specially for the children, and in which they may participate.

Christian Churches also offer help and advice to families through counselling and the running of such organisations as the Catholic Marriage Advisory Council and the Child Welfare Council. Churches may help Christian adults to look after their elderly parents through such organisations as the Methodist Homes for the Aged. Special meetings are run in some Churches to support elderly relatives, providing a place for them to have a meal and meet with friends.

Summary

- Christians see the family as very important for bringing up children to know what is good.
- There are several types of family, but Christians value marriage as the best basis for the family.
- Parents should take responsibility for teaching their children and children should respect their parents.
- Christian churches offer parents support in bringing up their family and encouraging children to become Christians.

3.7 Methods of contraception

Learning outcomes

By the end of this lesson you should be able to:

- give examples of contraception that are available
- explain why some people choose to use contraception
- give your own opinion and explain with reasons why you think this.

Natural method

Contraception is the deliberate prevention of pregnancy by natural or artificial methods. Advice on contraception is free and confidential. A natural method is the rhythm method, which means planning sexual intercourse around the woman's menstrual cycle to avoid the fertile time.

You learn how to record signals that you are fertile to identify when it is safer to have sex. Your GP can refer you to a family planning specialist teacher to learn how to use this method.

How effective it is depends on how carefully you follow the teaching and instructions. If followed carefully, it can be up to 98 per cent effective. It becomes very much less effective if the instructions are not followed or the menstrual cycle changes. This means that out of every hundred women using this carefully, two will have an unplanned pregnancy.

The benefits of the rhythm method are that there are no physical side-effects and it can be used to plan a pregnancy. However, it takes six months to learn your body's signals and these have to be recorded carefully every day. It does not protect you against sexually transmitted infections.

Artificial methods

There are a number of methods of artificial contraception to choose from and for most people in the UK they are free:

edexcel ::: key terms

Contraception – Intentionally preventing pregnancy from occurring.

- combined pill
- contraceptive implant
- contraceptive patch
- emergency contraception
- male and female condoms
- contraceptive injection
- diaphragms and caps
- intrauterine device or system (coil).

How effective the choice of contraceptive is depends on how carefully it is used. Implants and injections take away this risk.

Each form of contraception has its own benefits and side-effects. Diaphragms, caps and condoms offer protection from sexually transmitted diseases.

Why do people use contraception?

People use contraception because it allows them to choose when and if they want a baby. Some people may decide that having a baby is not for them because:

- they want to plan their own family in their own time
- they consider themselves to be too young or too old
- they do not believe they would be good parents
- becoming pregnant would be harmful to the health of the mother
- one or both partners carry a genetically inherited condition
- they feel they could not provide financially or emotionally for a child
- they have a lifestyle they feel would not be compatible with having a child
- in the case of a single man, he does not want to be responsible for a woman's pregnancy.

For discussion

The choice of method can be based around whether the contraception allows the egg to be fertilised. This then raises questions about whether life begins at conception and does contraception kill a potential life?

Activities

1   Research the different types of contraception available. Use the NHS websites.

2   Choose one type of contraception and explain why someone might choose this. What are the benefits and problems with using this?

3   Do you think it is the woman's responsibility to protect herself from pregnancy? Give reasons for your answer.

Sexually transmitted infections (STIs)

Sexually transmitted infections are passed on through intimate sexual contact. These include chlamydia, syphilis and gonorrhoea. In the UK, STIs have been rising continually since the 1990s. The highest increase in STIs has been among 16–24-year-olds.

Many STIs can be treated effectively if they are diagnosed in the early stages. However, if they are left untreated, they can cause long-term damage, illness and eventually death.

Having safe sex is the best way of preventing STIs. The male condom is the most effective method. However, you can never be 100 per cent sure that your partner does not have an STI and the more partners you have, the higher the risk of contracting an STI.

For discussion

Whose responsibility is it to protect you from STIs?

If everyone only had sex within long-term monogamous relationships, would this prevent STIs?

Summary

- Many people choose to use contraception so they can plan when to have their families.
- There are a variety of artificial methods available.

3.8 Christian attitudes to contraception and the reasons for them

Lesson outcomes

By the end of this lesson, you should be able to:

● outline different Christian attitudes towards contraception

● explain why there are different attitudes towards contraception within Christianity

● give your own opinion on the different attitudes with reasons for your answer.

Different Christian attitudes

Many people use contraception at some point in their lives but some religious believers are opposed to it.

Who	Believe what	Why
Roman Catholic and conservative evangelicals	Every sexual act should be open to the possibility of conception	• Using artificial methods of contraception is wrong because they prevent humans from fulfilling God's command to *'be fruitful and multiply'* (Genesis 1:28). • Sex was given by God for procreation and so every sexual act should allow for the possibility of conception to take place. • Contraception has encouraged promiscuity and the spread of sexually transmitted diseases. • The purpose of marriage is to have children. • These views have been upheld and reaffirmed by Popes.
The Church of England	Does not regard contraception as against God's plan	• The essence of Christianity is love, and contraception can be used to protect a woman's health. • Reducing the size of families gives children a better standard of living. • God created sex for pleasure and to provide an experience unique to the married couple. Contraception allows sex to be free from fear of pregnancy and provide the couple with safe pleasure. • There is nothing in the Bible that says contraception is wrong.

Activities

1 After considering the attitudes of Christians towards sex outside of marriage and the importance of having children and bringing them up in a stable family, do you think Christians should approve or disapprove of the use of contraception? Give reasons for your answer. What might someone who disagreed with you say?

2 Explain why there are different attitudes to contraception in Christianity.

ResultsPlus
Watch out!

Answers that receive lower marks will focus on general reasons why Christians may or may not allow contraception. Remember to include religious teachings in your answers.

For discussion

Whose responsibility should it be to decide to use contraception or not – the man's or the woman's?

Attitudes to different methods

The way in which the particular form of contraceptive actually stops pregnancy concerns some Christians. For most Christians, a barrier method (such as the cap or condom) is acceptable because the sperm and egg are prevented from meeting and so conception cannot take place. The conventional pill, which prevents conception by suppressing ovulation, is acceptable.

However, for many Christians, the coil and the morning after pill, which act after conception, and prevent implantation, are considered by some to be the equivalent to an abortion and are therefore unacceptable.

The use of contraception to protect against sexually transmitted diseases is one of the strongest arguments for its use, as sex in today's society poses a greater threat to people than pregnancy. From one act of unprotected sex a person could die of AIDS.

The Roman Catholic Church believes that every sexual act should be open to the possibility of conception.

> The prevention of a pregnancy is better than an abortion.

> *If people did not have sex outside marriage and followed the guidelines from the Church, there would be no need for the use of contraception.*

> The Catholic Church should reconsider its position on contraception, in the light of sexually transmitted diseases.

> *Contraception makes casual sex acceptable.*

Activities

3 Look at these statements expressing opinions about contraception. Do you agree with them? Give two reasons for each answer.

4 Create three more statements of your own and share them with a partner. Choose the one you agree with the most and say why.

5 Choose the one you disagree with the most and say why. Share your thoughts with your class.

ResultsPlus
Watch out!

Be aware of the spellings and differences between words that look similar – for example, conversion, conversation, conception and contraception.

Summary

- Most Christians today accept that some form of contraception is a responsible way of planning a family.
- Most also see children as a blessing from God but will allow that this does not mean having an unlimited number of children.
- Roman Catholic teaching holds that only a natural method of contraception is permissible, although more Catholics are now challenging this view.

For discussion

'It is better to use contraception than to have an unwanted baby.' Do you agree? Explain your opinion.

3.9 The media and marriage and the family

Learning outcomes

By the end of this lesson, you should be able to:

- research for yourself examples of media that cover issues from this topic
- identify the issue and say how it was covered
- explain, with examples, how this was fair or unfair to religious people or beliefs.

EastEnders

Coronation Street

Neighbours

Home and Away

HOLLYOAKS

Emmerdale

Issues in the media

In soaps, dramas, films, radio plays, and newspapers there are always stories about relationships, love, sex, marriage and, when things go wrong, divorce. These things are at the root of family life and society and make dramatic storylines.

Activities

1 Take a newspaper from today, read the stories carefully and use a highlighter to identify those that cover any of the issues raised in this section.

2 Take a magazine that explains what is happening next in the soaps, and do the same.

- How many examples of issues raised in this section can you find? Remember, it is anything to do with family, marriage, divorce, family planning.

- If you took out all of the storylines about these issues, what would be left? Would this be an interesting programme?

Activities

3 Look at the titles of TV soaps above. Which do you think is the odd one out? Why did you choose this?

- Do you think any of them are more realistic in their portrayal of family life?

- Do you think the views of Christians should be expressed in soap operas? Give reasons for your answer.

Take one issue – for example, 'sex outside marriage'. Sex before marriage is now represented in the soaps as the normal thing to do. It is expected that the characters will have sex before marriage and no one seems to be concerned about casual sex (promiscuity). In most storylines, the Christian attitude is not usually represented or, if it is, the Christian character is usually portrayed as someone who is out-of-touch with modern values and attitudes towards sex.

For discussion

'Soap operas are a good way of exploring serious issues about relationships.' Do you agree? What might someone argue who disagreed with you?

What you need to do to prepare for the exam

It is important to learn to look for things in storylines that are going to help you answer the examination questions.

- Watch the programme carefully, identify an issue that is covered.
- Look at the information about this issue from when you studied it. Identify what the different attitudes towards this issue are, including the non-religious ones.
- Now, watching the different characters in the storyline, identify which attitude they are representing. This is how the issue is being dealt with, explored through the characters and their points of view.
- Which attitudes were not covered?
- How could this storyline have been improved to cover all the different points of view?
- If the Christian point of view was covered, do you think the way the religious attitude was presented was fair to Christians?
- If the Christian attitude was not covered, how could it have been added?

TV and family life

In any soap opera there are many examples of different families. Some are nuclear families, others single parent or step families. If you go to the BBC *Eastenders* website there are family trees to explain how people are related to each other. Go to www.heinemann.co.uk/hotlinks express code 4202P for more information on *Eastenders* family trees. It would appear that the writers of *Eastenders* consider family an important part of any community. Family life offers the programme writers many opportunities to explore relationships, many of which we recognise from our own experience.

In Coronation Street, *Ken and Deirdre got married after a 20-year relationship.*

Activities

4   Do this exercise for a soap, a film and a newspaper report.

5   'Soap operas are a good way of exploring serious issues about relationships.'
   - Do you agree?
   - What might someone argue who disagreed with you?

6   Using a website from a popular soap opera, research how many different types of family you can identify.

7   Do you think each soap has different types of family represented?

Summary

- The media portray many issues surrounding marriage and the family.
- You need to evaluate two programmes to find evidence as to whether the way these issues are covered is fair to religious people.

examzone

Know Zone
Marriage and the family

Quick quiz

1 What word means making a promise before God in a wedding ceremony?
2 What is 'adultery'?
3 Suggest a social reason why a couple might cohabit.
4 Name two forms of artificial contraception.
5 What are the purposes of Christian marriage?
6 Why do many Christians oppose divorce?
7 Why does the Bible highlight the importance of the family?
8 How do Churches help families?
9 Why might Christians be against the use of contraception?
10 Name a soap opera storyline you could use in the exam for the Marriage and the family section.

Plenary activity

Create ideas maps for each of the lessons within this section. Remember to include:

- any 'facts' or laws that you need to know
- arguments for and against each issue
- Christian teachings on the issue
- different Christian opinions
- your own opinion with reasons.

Find out more

For a website containing information on Roman Catholic positions on all matters of interest to Catholics, try this hotlink: www.heinemann.co.uk/hotlinks (express code 4202P) and click on the appropriate link.

For an evangelical Christian website that explains the teaching on the role of the family today, go to www.heinemann.co.uk/hotlinks (express code 4202P) and click on the appropriate link.

Student tips

When I studied GCSE Religious Studies, I found this topic the hardest to appreciate as I felt that it presented a wrong picture of marriage and the family in society today. It just wasn't realistic because no one I know is in a religious family and the attitudes of some religious people to issues such as homosexuality, I think, is unacceptable. It wasn't until I visited one of my friends, who is a Christian, that I saw some people do take religion seriously and it does influence the way they live. It wouldn't suit me but it made me understand that there are good reasons for some people to live that way.

Self-evaluation checklist

Look at the following table. How would you rate your understanding of this topic? Use the following code to judge your status:

Green – I understand this fully.

Orange – I am confident I can answer most questions on this

Red – I need to do a lot more work on this topic.

Now answer the following questions:

- Do you hold an opinion on this topic and could you give reasons for that opinion if asked?
- Can you give the opinion of someone who disagrees with you and give reasons why they hold this opinion?

Content covered	My understanding is red/orange/green	Can I give my opinion?	Can I give an alternative opinion?
The changing attitudes to marriage, divorce, family life and homosexuality in the UK and the reasons for them.			
Christian attitudes to sex outside marriage and the reasons for them.			
The purposes of Christian marriage.			
The features of the Christian wedding ceremony and how this shows the purposes of marriage.			
Different Christian attitudes to divorce and the reasons for them.			
Different Christian attitudes to homosexuality and the reasons for them.			
Christian teachings on family life and its importance.			
How Christian Churches help with the raising of children and keeping families together.			
Different Christian attitudes to contraception and the reasons for them.			
How the media presents issues about marriage and family and whether their portrayal is fair to Christians.			

examzone

Know Zone
Marriage and the family

Introduction

In the exam you will see a choice of two questions on this section. Each question will include four tasks, which test your knowledge, understanding and evaluation of the material covered. A 2-mark question will ask you to define a term; a 4-mark question will ask your opinion on a point of view; an 8-mark question will ask you to explain a particular belief or idea; a 6-mark question will ask for your opinion on a point of view and ask you to consider an alternative point of view.

Give a glossary definition. You do not need to write any more – often this can be done in one sentence.

The 'explain why' questions are asking for you to give reasons. In this case the best way would be to give four reasons and explain them fully. It is possible to get to the highest level with two reasons but you must develop them fully. Once the examiner has awarded the level for your answer, they will look at the quality of your spelling and punctuation and use this to decide if you gain 7 or 8 marks. Be aware on the C questions to use formal English and check your spellings etc.

Mini exam paper

(a) What is **cohabitation**? (2 marks)

(b) Do you think divorce is better than an unhappy marriage? Give **two** reasons for your point of view. (4 marks)

(c) Explain why Christians are against sex outside marriage. (8 marks)

(d) 'No Christian should be homosexual.'
In your answer you should refer to Christianity.
   (i) Do you agree? Give reasons for your opinion. (3 marks)
   (ii) Give reasons why some people may disagree with you. (3 marks)

Give your opinion. Note, however, that marks are only awarded for the reasons you have for thinking that opinion is correct. Each reason needs to be explained to gain the marks available.

The (d) question is split into two parts – answer each part separately. You must refer to the statement and Christian beliefs during this whole question. It may be worth considering whether Christians would agree or disagree with this statement and use their reasons in (ii) and then provide the alternative point of view as your own.

   (i) You must give one very well-explained reason for your opinion or three simple reasons to gain full marks.

   (ii) You must now show that you understand the reasons that someone might disagree with you.

Mark scheme

(a) You will earn **2 marks** for a correct answer, and **1 mark** for a partially correct answer

(b) To earn up to the full **4 marks** you need to give two reasons (as asked) and to develop them fully. Two brief reasons will earn **2 marks** and one reason without development will earn **1 mark**.

(c) You can earn **7–8 marks** by giving up to four reasons, but the fewer reasons you give, the more you must develop them. You are being assessed on your use of language so you also need to take care to express your understanding in a clear style of English, and make some use of specialist vocabulary.

(d) To go beyond **3 marks** for the whole of this question, you must refer to Christianity. The more you are able to develop your reasons, the more marks you will earn. Three simple reasons can earn you the same mark as one fully developed reason.

ResultsPlus
Maximise your marks

(d) 'No Christian should be homosexual.'
  (i) Do you agree? Give reasons for your opinion. (3 marks)
  (ii) Give reasons why some people may disagree with you. (3 marks)

Student answer	Examiner comments	Improved student answer
(i) I disagree with the statement that no Christian should be homosexual, because God created all people and that means he created homosexuals too. If God created them, how can it be wrong?	The candidate gives their opinion with a reason and develops it. This would gain 2 marks. To gain full marks, the candidate needs to give a second reason or develop this one further, using the attitudes of the more liberal Christian groups.	(i) I disagree with the statement that no Christian should be homosexual because God created all people and that means he created homosexuals too. If God created them how can it be wrong? Also, being a Christian is about your spiritual life not your sexual life. There are also examples in the Bible of same-sex relationships that are admired by Christians such as David and Jonathan.
(ii) Some people may disagree with me because they think that God created male and female to procreate and that was his intention for life.	This is a 1-mark answer, giving a simple reason for the point of view.	(ii) Some people may disagree with me because they think that God created male and female to procreate and that was his intention for life. He created men and women to get married and have children. They also believe that homosexuality is not good for society as it undermines the family.

Religion and community cohesion

Introduction

In this section you will consider the issues that arise from humans being unique and different from each other. You will learn what Christians believe about how people should be treated and their attitudes towards gender roles, racism, prejudice and discrimination. You will understand how the teaching of the Bible and the Church promote racial harmony and community cohesion, and inspire Christians to work towards a peaceful and happy society. You will reflect on your own understanding of how to create equality and peace in the world.

Learning outcomes for this section

By the end of this section you will be able to:

- give definitions of the key terms and use them in answers to GCSE questions
- explain how and why attitudes to the roles of men and women have changed in the UK
- describe different Christian attitudes to equal rights for women in religion and explain the reasons for them
- explain how the UK works as a multi-ethnic society, and how it deals with problems of discrimination and racism
- explain how the government works to promote community cohesion in the UK, including legislation on equal rights for ethnic minorities and religions
- describe the work of a Christian church to help asylum seekers
- explain why Christians should help promote racial harmony
- outline the different Christian attitudes to other religions
- explain how the UK works as a multi-faith society and outline the benefits of living in a multi-faith society
- identify the issues raised for religion by a multi-faith society
- describe the ways in which religions work to promote community cohesion in the UK.

edexcel ::: key terms

community cohesion	interfaith marriage	prejudice	religious freedom
discrimination	multi-ethnic society	racial harmony	religious pluralism
ethnic minority	multi-faith society	racism	sexism

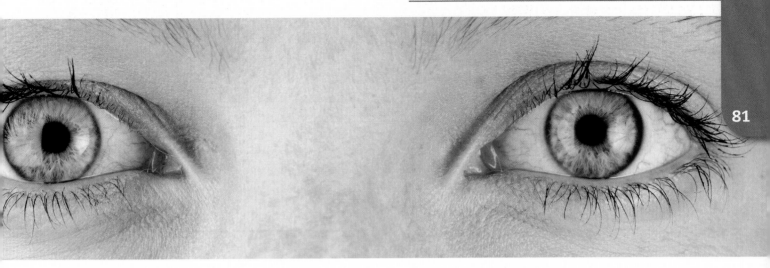

What if we were judged on the colour of our eyes?

Consider what the consequences would be if tomorrow scientists decided that medical evidence proved beyond a shadow of a doubt that blue-eyed people were ultimately better at everything!

How long would it take before a difference between blue-eyed and brown-eyed people began to develop? What would be the first changes? Take it a step further... make a flowchart of how things would develop.

Think about these ideas:

- Would it really be worth spending money educating brown-eyed people?
- If they were not educated, what jobs could they get?
- Eventually how would society be divided?
- Would the brown-eyed people end up living in one area?
- Why might this happen?
- Would it be better to restrict their movements so they only came out of this area to work?
- How would the brown-eyed people feel?
- What would you do if you had blue eyes?
- At the very end of your chart consider, if the brown-eyed people are inferior and are uneducated or unable to work, they only cause problems for the blue-eyed people. Is it worth considering 'reducing' the number of brown-eyed people, or removing them completely?

Final thought: 'Is this right?'

4.1 Government action to promote community cohesion

Learning outcomes

By the end of this lesson, you should be able to:

● give the reasons for racism in the UK in past times

● give examples of government measures to combat racism

● explain the importance of racial equality and community cohesion.

● give your own opinion, with reasons on issues, of community cohesion.

edexcel ▦ key terms

Community cohesion – A common vision and shared sense of belonging for all groups in society.

Religious freedom – The right to practise your religion and change your religion.

What is community cohesion?

Government legislation covers six key areas: gender, race, disability, age, faith and belief, and sexual orientation. **Community cohesion** means different communities living together and sharing four things in common:

● a common vision and sense of belonging

● appreciating and valuing the differences between people of different cultures

● ensuring equal opportunities for all in the community

● making strong and positive relationships with people of different races.

The government has put in place measures and legislation to promote community cohesion and to try to prevent prejudice and discrimination.

The action from the government includes:

● practical support on cohesion

● a new interfaith strategy that focuses on what needs to be done to promote interaction and dialogue between faiths

● funding for local authorities to respond to problems such as immigration, and to encourage links between groups from different backgrounds through youth projects, school or places of worship twinning programmes, local pride in the community campaigns and meetings for conflict resolution

Activities

1 Research your local authority website to find out what has been put in place to promote community cohesion.

In recent years the government has passed laws to protect **religious freedom**. These laws include the:

● Employment Equality (Religion or Belief) Regulations 2003

● Racial and Religious Hatred Act 2006

● Equality Act 2006 (part 2 2007)

● Human Rights Act 1998.

- citizenship days throughout the UK to celebrate national and local culture and stress the sharing of local traditions and such British values as respect for the rule of law, tolerance and democracy
- information packs for new migrants that set out their rights and responsibilities
- specialist integration teams and cohesion teams to help local councils manage any major changes in the local population
- support with translation and learning the English language for those who do not speak English.

(Adapted from 'Blears's £50 million investment in community cohesion.')

The government describes an equal society as:

'*An equal society protects and promotes equal freedom and substantive opportunity to live in the way people value and would choose so everyone can flourish. An equal society recognises people's different needs, situations and goals and removes the barriers that limit what people can do and be.*'
(Fairness and Freedom: The Final Report of the Equalities Review, HMSO 2007)

Activities

2 Do you think the passing of laws can prevent prejudice and discrimination? Give reasons for your answer.

3 What else do you think the government should do to promote community cohesion?

4 Your school has policies on equality. Find out what these are and how they are monitored. As a member of the school community, how can you help to promote community cohesion?

⇨ Find out more

Find out more about the Commission for Racial Equality and their work on community cohesion: go to www.heinemann.co.uk/hotlinks (express code 4202P) and click on the appropriate link.

For a community cohesion website with lots of links to other community cohesion sites: go to www.heinemann.co.uk/hotlinks (express code 4202P) and click on the appropriate link.

I have recently been forced to move to the UK by my parents. My father has been asked to manage a large British company and we all had to move with him. I was really excited, in school at home we were taught how the UK was a wonderful place to live. I had seen TV soap programmes (like *EastEnders* and *Coronation Street*) where people from other countries had arrived and been accepted.

But this is not the case. We moved into a road where no one speaks to us, someone put an awful note through our letter box and my mum cried for days. My father's car had its tyres let down and we dare not go out.

At school I am called names and no one wants to be my friend. They claim my father took a job off someone and I should go back where I came from… I am so unhappy…

Tomorrow we are going to go to a local church, I hope to find a friend there…

Summary

- The government is committed to promoting community cohesion and has introduced measures and laws to prevent discrimination.

4.2 Changing attitudes to the roles of men and women in the UK

84

edexcel ::: key terms

Discrimination – Treating people less favourably because of their ethnicity/gender/colour/sexuality/age/class.

Prejudice – Believing some people are inferior or superior without even knowing them.

Sexism – Discriminating against people because of their gender (being male or female).

Glossary

Equality – The state of everyone having equal rights regardless of their gender, race or class.

A woman's role?

Until quite recently, most people thought that a woman's role in society was to stay at home and look after the children. It was only in 1918 that women in the UK were allowed to vote and it was not until 1970 that women were given the right to equal pay with men. Women's roles in society have changed dramatically along with their legal rights. Now, in the 21st century, women's lives are very different. However, do they really have equality with men?

In recent years, the traditional role of men has changed significantly too. Many men take a much more active role in the raising of children and the care of the home. Men are much more willing to cook and do the tasks that used to be seen as 'women's work'.

Activities

1   Look at the different images of women on page 84. Which is the odd one out and why?

2   Reorder the pictures to show how women have changed over the years. What makes you think they have changed? What has changed? Do women now have equal rights to men?

ResultsPlus
Watch out!

Some candidates focus on the history of women's rights. This is important but it is equally important to mention the inequalities that still remain.

Progress?

A century ago only 15 per cent of married women worked outside the home. However, after the two world wars, attitudes changed. During the Second World War women did the work of the men who had gone to fight in war. After the war ended, women's organisations campaigned for equal rights and women were reluctant to give up their jobs and independence.

Some people, however, still believed that men should remain the provider and therefore should be paid more for the work they did. Many also believed that family life would be spoiled if the mother worked and did not stay at home with the children.

The introduction of the contraceptive pill gave women the choice whether to have a family or not, and the opportunity to pursue a career. As more women made the choice to work and were successful, and in many cases still raised a family, it became more accepted by society.

Activities

3   Outline how the roles of women have changed in the UK in recent years. What evidence do you have for this?

4   Explain why some people think that women still do not have equal rights with men?

5   Do you think men and women can have equal rights? Explain why.

In the UK today, women and men have equal rights in law. However, many would claim that inequality still exists. For example, recent surveys have shown that the jobs available to women are often less well-paid, so that men still earn around 17 per cent more than women. Also, the traditional roles still exist, with women doing the majority of household chores and childcare. In the workplace, jobs such as nursing are still seen as 'female' and there are far fewer women than men in positions of real power or influence. Cases of **discrimination** and **prejudice** against women (**sexism**) still occur.

Activities

6   Do you think that men should be allowed equal right to time off when a child is born? Give two reasons for your answer.

7   War, the introduction of the contraceptive pill and a woman's right to work have contributed to the change in attitudes to women. Which do you think had the most effect and why?

Summary

- The roles of men and women have changed over the last hundred years, since the Suffragette movement until the present day.

- The law provides for equal opportunities in employment but some people think there are still inequalities in practice.

- Some problems still remain to be solved.

4.3 Christian attitudes to equal rights for women in the Church

Learning outcomes

By the end of this lesson you should be able to:

- describe and explain why there are different attitudes to the role of women in the Church
- give your own opinion as to whether women should be leaders in the Church, with reasons.

> *There is neither Jew nor Greek, there is neither bond nor free, there is neither male nor female: for ye are all one in Christ Jesus.*
> Galatians 3.28

> *Women should remain silent in the churches. They are not allowed to speak, but must be in submission, as the law says.*
> 1 Corinthians 14:34

> *Submitting yourself one to another in fear of God.*
> Ephesians 5:21 (paraphrased)

> *So God created man in his own image, in the image of God created he him; male and female created he them.*
> Genesis 1:27

Activities

1 What do the Bible verses opposite tell you about the role of women in religion in biblical times?

For discussion

Why didn't Jesus have female disciples? What was Jesus's attitude towards the women he met?

Christians today believe that men and women should have equal rights, although their roles (what they do) may be different. One area where there is still a lot of disagreement is whether women should become priests or Church leaders. It has only been in the last few years that women have been allowed to become priests in the Church of England, and they are still not allowed in the Roman Catholic Church.

Activities

2 Complete the final row in the chart on page 87. What do you think about women priests?

3 Why do Christians have different attitudes towards the role of women in church?

A female priest.

Christian attitudes to women priests

Who	What	Why
Traditional evangelical Protestants	Men should be the head of the family and women should not speak in church or be ministers or priests	• St Paul's statements in the Bible about women not being allowed to speak in church, and having to submit to their husbands. • Their belief that the Bible is the unalterable word of God.
Liberal Christians, many Protestant Churches, e.g. the Church of England, Methodist, United Reform Church	Men and women should have equal roles in life including religion and so allow women priests	• St Paul said 'There is neither… male nor female for you are all one person in Christ.' • Jesus treated women as equals and had women followers like Martha and Mary. • Jesus's women followers were the only people to stay with him during his crucifixion and Mary Magdalene was first person to see him when he rose from the dead. • They believe that Jesus chose men as his apostles because of the culture of the time and not for any theological reasons.
Roman Catholics	Men and women should have equal roles because men and women have equal status in the eyes of God. However, only men can become priests.	• Jesus only chose men to be his successors. • Jesus was a man and the priest represents Jesus in the Mass.
I think…	that	because

ResultsPlus
Build better answers

Explain different Christian attitudes to the role of women. (8 marks)

 Basic, 0–2 mark answers

These answers will only offer one correct attitude.

 Good, 3–6 mark answers

These answers will mention some of the various opinions within Christianity either about the role of women in society or in the Church.

 Excellent, 7–8 mark answers

The highest marks will be given to answers that include a variety of opinions and identify which types of Christians are most likely to believe what. For example, traditional Christians believe that men should provide for women and a woman's role is in raising a family only. Higher level answers will include opinions about the role of women in the various Christian Churches as well as in society. For example, 'Roman Catholics believe that men and women should have equal roles but they do not allow women priests because…'

For discussion

What advantages does each gender have if they are appointed as priests?

Summary

- The Bible teaches that men and women are created equal and Jesus used women a great deal in his ministry.
- The teaching of St Paul seems to suggest certain inequalities.
- The Church of England has allowed the ordination of women priests since 1994, though this has been very controversial.
- Some other Churches, including the Roman Catholic Church, forbid the ordination of women.

4.4 The UK as a multi-ethnic society

Learning outcomes

By the end of this lesson, you should be able to:

- outline what is meant by a multi-ethnic society
- describe how the UK has become multi-ethnic
- suggest advantages and disadvantages in living in a multi-ethnic society
- give a reasoned opinion about the issues.

edexcel ⠿ key terms

Ethnic minority – A member of an ethnic group (race) which is much smaller than the majority group.

Multi-ethnic society – Many different races and cultures living together in one society.

Racism – The belief that some races are superior to others.

A multi-ethnic society

The UK is a **multi-ethnic society**, which means that it is made up of many different races, cultures and nationalities living together in one society. Many people in the UK today are worried about immigration (people moving into the country from overseas). However, the UK has always been a land of many races: from the Romans of 2,000 years ago, through to the Saxons, the Normans and the many others who have settled here. Some immigrants come to find a better life, or to work, while others come to find safety from fear of death at home.

In 1991, the government carried out a census to discover how many different ethnic groups there were in the UK. The pie chart shows the main results. The small slices represent each **ethnic minority**.

More recently, there has been large-scale immigration to the UK from the countries of eastern Europe, particularly Poland. These countries recently joined the European Union, giving their citizens the right to work in other European Union countries. Between 2004 and 2006, for example, there were more than 600,000 eastern Europeans who came to live and work in the UK. Most work either in the building or retail industries. However, there have been protests about the pressure the new immigrants have brought on housing and other public services.

During the same time period, 198,000 British citizens emigrated (moved out of the country). Most of these people went to live in southern Europe, Australia or New Zealand.

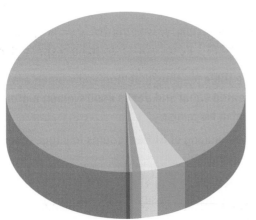

Key

- White British
- Asian/Asian British
- Black/Black British
- Mixed race
- Chinese
- Other ethnic groups

The ethnic make-up of the total population of the UK.

Activities

1 Study the pie chart.
   a) Which is the largest ethnic group in the UK?
   b) What is the largest non-white group? Why do you think this is?
   c) What do you think this tells us about multi-ethnic society in the UK?
   d) Do you think it is right that citizens of the European Union should be able to work in other countries? What are the advantages and disadvantages?

There are many advantages to living in a multi-ethnic society:

- It helps people of different races and cultures to understand one another better.
- It enables us to understand different religions.
- It gives us a wider variety of music, food, clothes and culture.
- It can bring new people with fresh ideas.

The Brixton race riots in 1981.

The Notting Hill Carnival.

Racism and discrimination

One of the serious problems that can occur in a multi-ethnic society is **racism**. Racism is the belief that certain ethnic groups are superior to others. This has led to many people being treated badly and their human rights not being respected just because of their nationality or the colour of their skin. For example, not many years ago, there were race riots in the UK caused by unemployment and poor social conditions.

Summary

- The UK is a multi-ethnic society.
- This has caused racial problems, which have gradually lessened over the years until the situation is much better today.
- Being a multi-ethnic society has many advantages, especially concerned with understanding and appreciating different cultures and beliefs.

4.5 Why Christians should promote racial harmony

Learning outcomes

By the end of this lesson, you should be able to:

● outline biblical teaching on racial harmony

● explain why Christians should work to promote racial harmony.

Christian teachings

Christianity is opposed to racism. The Bible teaches that all races are equal in the eyes of God:

> For God created man in his own image.
> Genesis 1:27

> God does not show favouritism, but accepts men from every nation.
> Acts 10:34–35

> There is neither Jew nor Greek... you are all one in Christ.
> Galatians 3:28

> Love your neighbour as yourself.
> Luke 10:27

Jesus always treated people the same, no matter where they were from. For example, he healed a Roman's servant (Luke 7:1–10) and, in the parable of the Good Samaritan, taught that people of different races and ethnic groups should not hate each other, but should follow God's command to love one another. This is known as **racial harmony**.

Activities

1 Explain what is meant by the phrase 'God created man in his own image'. How do you explain that there are also women, and a wide variety of types of people all different in some way?

2 What does Jesus mean when he says 'Love your neighbour as yourself'? Is this possible?

3 What other reasons might there be for promoting racial harmony?

edexcel ⋮⋮⋮ key terms

Racial harmony – Different races/ colours living together happily.

For discussion

Do you think the Christian Church has done enough to combat racism? Give reasons for your answer.

Barack Obama was elected as President of the USA in November 2008.

Christianity and racial harmony today

Today, Christian Churches throughout the world condemn racism and encourage all Christians to treat everyone equally.

Recently, the first ever black President of America was elected. This has made history. Many people think this is a sign that racism is less present in the modern world than it was 50 years ago, and could be eliminated within the next 50 years. They trace the beginnings of this to 28 August 1963 when, in a speech, Martin Luther King said he had a dream that one day black people and white people would live equally together in peace.

For discussion

What is the solution to racism? How can we achieve this?

The Methodist Church regards racism as a direct contradiction of the gospel of Jesus. According to the Catechism of the Catholic Church, '*Every form of social and cultural discrimination must be curbed and eradicated as incompatible with God's design.*'

ResultsPlus
Exam question report

Explain why Christians should help to promote racial harmony. (8 marks) June 2007

How students answered

Most students did poorly on this question. Most of these candidates answered in general terms as to why people should promote racial harmony and not Christians specifically.

Some students gave a few reasons why Christians should promote racial harmony but did not support this fully or go into detail.

A few candidates who produced excellent answers supported the reasons for Christians promoting racial harmony with biblical teachings and the example of Jesus.

Summary

- The Bible teaches that racism is wrong and that all people are equal.
- Martin Luther King is one of the many Christians who have fought against racism.
- The Christian Church works to encourage social harmony.

4.6 The work of one Christian church to help people who are seeking asylum

Learning outcomes

By the end of this lesson, you should be able to:

- describe the work of one Christian church that is working with people seeking asylum
- explain why Christians should help people seeking asylum
- give your opinion on the support given to people seeking asylum and your reasons for holding this view.

Glossary

Asylum seeker – Someone who formally requests permission to live in another country because they (and often their families) have a 'well-founded fear of persecution' in their country of origin.

A person who is seeking asylum is someone who is fleeing persecution in their homeland. They arrive at another country and make themselves known to the authorities and ask for asylum. Once asylum has been granted and they are allowed to stay, they become a refugee.

A migrant worker is a person who migrates from one country to another to get work. Migrant workers can come from all over the world, including Australia, India, South Africa and, more recently, the countries that joined the European Union in 2004, which includes Poland and Lithuania as well as others. Because we live in a global economy, many organisations encourage people to work or study in the UK.

Collectively, these people add to the culture and diversity of a region, enriching life in the UK for everyone.

Assist Sheffield

Assist stands for Asylum Seeker Support Initiative – Short Term. Assist is a charity that helps destitute asylum seekers in and around Sheffield. Asylum seekers become destitute when all the support they have been receiving from the government is withdrawn when they do not achieve asylum. After this they are not allowed to work and many struggle daily for food, accommodation and clothing. It is estimated that there are about 1,000 destitute asylum seekers in the Sheffield area alone who are being denied access to homeless shelters or any state-funded support.

Assist tries to help the situation by:

- finding night shelter for those who are sleeping rough
- finding temporary accommodation with host families and houses on loan
- paying a small weekly grant for food and basic living expenses

Activities

1 There are many stories about people seeking asylum and migrant workers that are believed by some. For example:

- 'They take our homes.'
- 'They are lazy.'
- 'They get houses and are given new cookers, fridges and washers free.'
- 'They are taking our jobs.'

Find out if these stories are true. Research what asylum seekers are entitled to in your local area.

- advising about other sources of assistance available (charitable and non-charitable)
- giving free bus pass vouchers to those with serious medical problems and pregnant women who would find it difficult to walk
- giving free bicycles
- finding long-term solutions by helping people to keep asking for asylum
- raising awareness about the problem through events and talks.

Assist relies very much on the generosity of the public of all faiths to meet the basic living needs of asylum seekers, although it depends on Christians in particular for its support. So far, they have been able to help over 60 destitute asylum seekers each week with grants; about 25 of these are also provided with accommodation. When making decisions about who should be helped, they try to give priority to those who suffer serious medical problems as well as to women in the late stages of pregnancy. Those who cannot be helped still benefit a lot from advice given by volunteers about how they can access other forms of assistance. (Text adapted from Assist website.)

⇨ Find out more

Find out more about the work of Assist Sheffield from their website. Go to www.heinemann.co.uk/hotlinks (express code 4202P) and click on the appropriate link.

One local church in Sheffield that works with Assist is St Thomas Church, Sheffield. It has a project called 'The Open Hands Project'. Find out about the Open Hands Project run by St Thomas Church, Sheffield. Go to www.heinemann.co.uk/hotlinks (express code 4202P) and click on the appropriate link.

ResultsPlus
Watch out!

You will get credit for any relevant examples you use in the exam – in this case make sure that you find out as much as you can about the work of at least one Christian church for asylum seekers.

Why should Christians help people who are seeking asylum?

One of Jesus's most important teachings about helping others was in the parable of the Sheep and Goats (Matthew 25:31–46). In this, Jesus said God would judge people on the way they treated each other.

'When I was hungry you fed me, I was thirsty and you gave me a drink: I was a stranger and you received me in your homes, I was naked and you clothed me; I was sick and you took care of me, I was in prison and you visited me.' He explained that 'Whenever you did that for one of the least important of these brothers of mine, you did it for me.'

Activities

2 Explain why the parable of the sheep and goats might cause Christians to help asylum seekers.

3 Do you think this work is important?

4 Investigate one church in your local area that does this sort of work and produce a package of information about their work. Give examples of what they do, its importance and significance.

5 Interview some people seeking asylum in your area. Ask them about where they have come from and why. Ask how they have been treated and whether they have encountered prejudice and discrimination. How do you feel about this?

Summary

- Many Christians try to help asylum seekers because of the teachings of Jesus.
- Christian churches such as St Thomas Church in Sheffield run projects to help asylum seekers.

4.7 The UK as a multi-faith society

Learning outcomes

By the end of this lesson, you should be able to:

- outline what is meant by a multi-faith society
- describe how the UK has become multi-faith
- suggest advantages and disadvantages in living in a multi-faith society
- give a reasoned opinion about the issues.

The UK is made up of people of many different races, cultures and religions.

The UK:

- is a multi-faith society (people of different religious faiths and beliefs live alongside one another)
- accepts religious pluralism (all faiths have an equal right to co-exist)
- offers religious freedom to everyone (members of all religions are free to worship).

edexcel ⦂⦂ key terms

Multi-faith society – Many different religions living together in one society.

Activities

1 Draw an ideas map of the advantages of a multi-faith society. It might help if you think about your work on the advantages of a multi-ethnic society.

The benefits of a multi-faith society

Being a **multi-faith society** has given the UK:

- a varied and rich cultural life
- a better understanding of different cultures and viewpoints
- a greater tolerance and understanding of other ways of life
- new ways of living and enjoying life, e.g. yoga, meditation, dance.

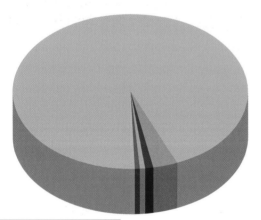

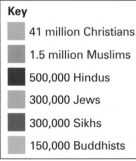

Key
- 41 million Christians
- 1.5 million Muslims
- 500,000 Hindus
- 300,000 Jews
- 300,000 Sikhs
- 150,000 Buddhists

The main religious groups in the UK in 2001.

The Archbishop of Canterbury, Rowan Williams, and the Dalai Lama meeting.

For discussion

What religions do the leaders shown on page 94 represent? Do you think that such meetings are helpful? Say why.

Activities

2 List the reasons why people may think that the UK does not treat members of all religions equally.

Religious freedom means that religious groups from all over the world can live peacefully together. It means that people are able to understand other religions and are less worried about people who are different from themselves, which in the past has been a major cause of prejudice and tension.

Think of the variety and diversity of a garden with lots of different flowers of all colours and species. This makes a wonderful, interesting and exciting garden.

The challenges presented by a multi-faith society

It also challenges people to think more about their own faith and to be more open and understanding of the views of others. Hopefully, such understanding will lead to less fear and less religious persecution in the future. It has not been easy for the UK to become a multi-faith society and there is still a great deal of religious tension in certain areas. For instance, many religious believers feel that religious tolerance has led to many of their beliefs and values being ignored.

Summary

- There are many different faiths in the UK. All people are free to follow whatever religion they wish.

- The advantages of a multi-faith society are that people are free to worship and this helps people to understand one another better.

- Some people believe that this causes religious tension and that some religious values are being ignored.

4.8 Differences among Christians in their attitudes to other religions

Learning outcomes

By the end of this lesson, you should be able to:

● explain what is meant by the terms exlusivism, inclusivism, and pluralism

● describe the different Christian attitudes to other religions and the reasons for this

● give your own opinion on the issues raised by Christians and other religions, with reasons for your answer.

edexcel ▦ key terms

Religious pluralism – Accepting all religions as having an equal right to coexist.

Glossary

Religious exclusivism – Belief that true Christians will go to Heaven and others will be excluded.

Religious inclusivism – Belief that all religions lead to God but that Christianity is the only religion with the full truth.

What attitudes do Christians have towards other faiths?

Activities

1 List some of the reasons why Christians might give for saying that only their religion is right.

2 Do you think that if you believe you only have the answer through Christianity, you should try to convert others? Give reasons for your answer.

3 Should Christians become missionaries? Give reasons for your answer.

Exclusive, inclusive or pluralist

It is generally accepted by everyone, including most Christians, that people should be free to follow whatever religion they like, or none at all. There are, however, three different Christian attitudes to religious freedom: religious exclusivism, religious inclusivism and **religious pluralism**.

Christian attitudes to religious freedom

Who	What	Why
Evangelical or exclusive Christians	Believe that true Christians (those with a personal relationship with God through Jesus) will go to Heaven and everyone else will be excluded	Jesus said, 'I am the way, the truth and the life; no one will come to the father except through me' (John 14:6).
Roman Catholic Christians or inclusive Christians	Believe that while all religions can help people to reach God, Christianity is the only religion with the full truth	Jesus taught that people who believe in him get into Heaven, and only Christians believe Jesus is the Son of God. This means that other faiths should be respected but encouraged to convert to Christianity. 'The Catholic Church recognises in other religions that search, among shadows and images, for the God who is unknown yet near.' (Catechism of the Catholic Church)
Pluralist Christians	Believe all religions will lead to God, they are all equal and no one is wrong	Jesus never tried to convert the Jews, and he said 'in my father's house there are many rooms, and I am going to prepare a place for you' (John 14:2). This is thought to mean that there is room for all religions.

ResultsPlus
Exam question report

Explain why there are different Christian attitudes towards other religions. (8 marks)

How students answered

Many candidates scored poorly on this question because they were confused by the question and did not address the issue of other religions in their answers.

Most of the candidates who scored 3–6 marks for this question described the different Christian attitudes (exclusivism, inclusivism and pluralism) but did not explain why these beliefs were held in any detail.

There were a few excellent answers that described all three viewpoints within Christianity giving examples of groups that held this belief, and then went on to explain why, backing up their answers with religious teachings.

A Christian missionary working in Argentina.

Summary

- There are three types of attitudes held by Christians about religious freedom: exclusive, inclusive and pluralist.
- All of these attitudes are supported through religious teachings.

4.9 Issues raised about multi-faith societies

Learning outcomes

By the end of this lesson, you should be able to:

- explain what a multi-faith society is
- state some of the advantages of a multi-faith society
- state some problems with a multi-faith society
- evaluate the advantages and problems, and express your own opinions.

Most religious believers in the UK accept that people should be allowed to follow whatever religion they like. However, others are not so sure and others say that only their religion is right and that everyone should follow it.

Living in a society that has many different religious followers within it raises some issues for believers. This is particularly true when it comes to conversion, the upbringing of children and **interfaith marriage**.

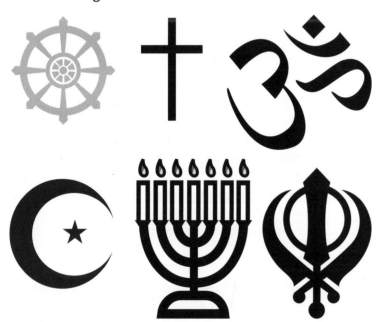

Symbols of the six main world religions.

For discussion

Can all faiths be right?

edexcel ::: key terms

Interfaith marriage – Marriage where the husband and wife are from different religions.

Activities

1 Describe what is meant by a multi-faith society.
2 List some of the reasons why Christians might give for saying their religion is the only right one.

Conversion

When believers from different religions live together in one place there can be some issues if one religious group tries to convert another. If you believe your religion has the answer, and is correct, then you may feel that the right thing to do is to share this with other people and, however good the intention, this can cause conflict. The disagreement or conflict may stem from the implication that one set of beliefs is better than another, thus causing offence.

For discussion

Should members of religious faiths try to covert others to their faith? Is it acceptable to try to convert someone who does not follow any religion?

ResultsPlus
Build better answers

Explain why trying to convert people may cause problems in a multi-faith society. (8 marks)

 Basic, 0–2 mark answers
Basic answers only focus on one reason or offer a variety of reasons without explaining them.

 Good, 3–6 mark answers
These answers will offer one or two (for Level 3) developed reasons or may offer many reasons without explaining them.

 Excellent, 7–8 mark answers
The best answers will offer many reasons and fully explain at least two of them. The main reason used in better answers is that conversion implies that one religion is better than another, which is against the idea of an equal multi-faith society. The candidate will use some key terms and good English.

Interfaith marriage and the bringing up of children

If two members of different religions fall in love and marry, it could be the beginnings of a union that helps the two faith communities understand one another. In some cases it is a very positive happening. In other cases, conflict can be caused as the families disagree on whether a couple can live together happily when the core values they hold and the beliefs they follow are different. In many religions, marrying someone outside the faith is frowned upon and even banned because marriage is regarded as the basis for bringing children up within the faith. The mixture of beliefs and faiths can lead to confusion.

- Can the parents agree on how to bring up the children?
- What religion will their children belong to?
- How will their children be raised?
- Which religious festivals will they observe?
- Which religious community will the family belong to?

Activities

3 Draw an ideas map of the advantages and disadvantages of a multi-faith marriage.

For discussion

A marriage will be happiest if the couple belong to the same faith. Do you agree? Say why, or why not.

Problems arising in the UK

There have been problems arising from the multi-faith nature of the society in the UK. There have been a number of violent interfaith clashes and many difficult questions have been raised. Many people have argued that the UK is still a predominantly Christian country, not a multi-faith one, and that Christian traditions, such as Christmas, should remain an important part of UK life.

Summary

- There are problems concerning religious freedom in a multi-faith society.
- Some people believe that the UK is a Christian country, not a multi-faith one.
- There are issues about multi-faith marriages.

4.10 Ways in which religions work to promote community cohesion

Learning outcomes

By the end of this lesson, you should be able:

- understand more about what a multi-faith society is
- explain the problems of having faiths together
- give your opinion on how life has changed in the UK since it became a multi-faith society.

Religious harmony

If members of different religions are to live harmoniously together, they need to work hard to promote friendship and community cohesion. To do this, people of all faiths have to:

- listen to each others' views
- learn to live and work together
- respect each others' faith
- share common values, such as tolerance, respect, charity and non-violence.

Activities

1 Religions all seem to have some shared values and beliefs. Make a list of these values and beliefs. Do you think all religions have a lot more in common than they have differences? Give reasons for your answer.

Groups that help community cohesion

Religious groups such as the Council of Christians and Jews and the Inter Faith Network for the UK, have been working together in recent years to heal divisions between different faiths. They work on the basis that God created all humanity to have a relationship with him. Some religious believers even suggest that all who believe in God should be united in a single faith and that terms such as 'Christian' and 'Muslim' should no longer be used.

Shared festivals

Another way in which community cohesion may be achieved is where people of different faiths share their festivals together. However, some people have complained that certain city councils believe that celebrating Christmas in a public way may be offensive to non-Christians and are refusing to put up Christmas signs and instead are calling it a 'Winter Festival'. Those opposed to this say that it excludes Christianity.

Activities

2 Do you think that Christmas should be renamed 'the Winter Festival'? Give reasons for your view.

A seasonal greeting card may be used instead of a Christmas card.

Faith schools

Another way in which community cohesion can be helped is through faith schools. These schools are run on religious lines. At the moment, in the state system there are 21,000 schools, of which 6580 are Christian-based, with 37 Jewish, 7 Islamic and 2 Sikh schools. The government has promised to support the establishment of more schools of different faiths in order to improve educational standards and understanding among the various

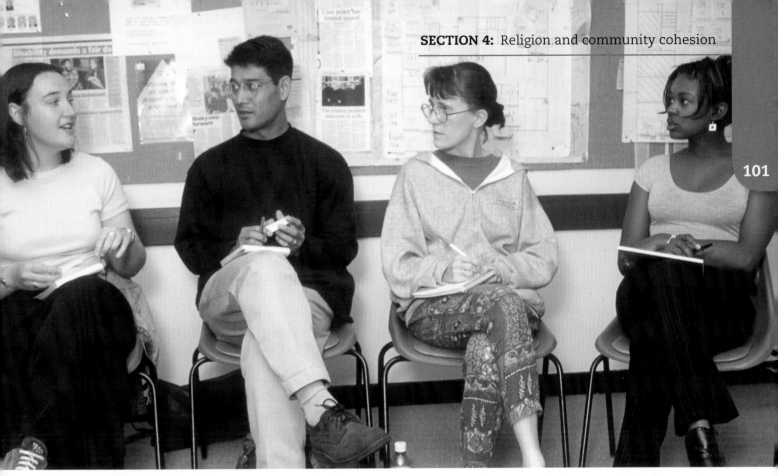

Young people from different backgrounds working together.

religious communities. However, opponents of faith schools claim that they are exclusive to that religion and do not give their students an all-round understanding of other faiths.

The opponents also argue that if we are to achieve community cohesion and learn to live together

peacefully, this would be best achieved in mixed faith schools.

In the UK there are many multi-faith groups that work together to promote community cohesion. In every authority there is a group called the Standing Advisory Council for Religious Education (SACRE). This group meets to agree on what should be taught in Religious Education in local schools and ways in which they can support teaching and learning. The members of the group are people from all the faiths represented in the area. They work together to provide a syllabus that encourages understanding of the faiths. Some local authorities have youth SACREs where young people from different faiths meet together to discuss how to promote understanding between the faith groups.

For discussion

'Faith schools hinder, rather than help community cohesion.' Do you agree? Give your reasons.

Activities

3 Outline ways in which religions work to promote community cohesion.

4 Research in your area religious groups that work together to promote community cohesion.

5 Look through a recent newspaper. Are there any articles about groups working to promote community cohesion? Who is involved in the group?

Summary

- Religious groups in the UK are working hard to establish community cohesion.
- There are still a number of problems and issues to be resolved.

4.11 Religion and community cohesion in the media

Learning outcomes

By the end of this lesson, you should be able to:

- explain how different forms of media tackle community cohesion

- describe examples of storylines in newspapers, films or the national press that cover a matter raised in this section

- give evidence from the media to explain whether the coverage was fair or unfair to religious people

- evaluate the importance of the media being sensitive and accurate when reporting issues concerning community cohesion.

The soaps

In soap operas, programme writers often use the storyline to promote understanding or air an issue that society as a whole is grappling with at the time. These may become some of the most moving and interesting storylines in the soaps. They may include stories about racial prejudice and tension, the way a religious family comes to live within a local community without compromising their beliefs, and domestic violence towards women or the treatment of women in general.

Activities

1 List all the storylines that cover community cohesion that have appeared in soaps or dramas in recent years.

2 Do you watch TV documentaries, discussion programmes (e.g. *Big Questions*) or listen to radio programmes that explore moral issues? Give your reasons for your answer.

3 Are women, religious people and people from other ethnic groups represented fairly on TV? Give reasons for your answer.

Issues of religion and community cohesion are often highlighted through TV dramas and films or soaps.

The first episode in *The Vicar of Dibley*, 'The Arrival', explores the different attitudes towards women priests through the points of view of the different characters. Initially, the community is divided by her arrival. However, as time goes on and they get to know her, their ideas change.

Activities

4   Choose one issue from this section (the role of women in the Church, people seeking asylum or migrant workers, racism, or multi-faith issues) and write your own storyline for a TV soap or drama. Give each character something to say that shows their attitude towards the issue and allow them to explain why they hold it. Present this in the form of a spider diagram with the issue at the centre. Check you have included what Christians do or say about the issue.

How fair is your storyline to the viewpoint of religious people? Does the character represent their beliefs in a positive way?

ResultsPlus
Watch out!

You have been introduced to how the media covers religious or moral issues. You will be asked throughout the sections of the examination to give examples of media you have seen, read or listened to. The questions will usually be 'Explain how the issue was covered' and 'Is the treatment of the issue fair or unfair to religious people?' Or it might be a 'Do you think?' question.

Activities

5   Complete the following chart for sections 2–4 (section 1 is slightly different). Write in detail – this will be a summary ready for your revision.

Section	One example of media storyline/ article and how it covered the issue	Was if fair/unfair to religious beliefs/ people? Give reasons
2 Matters of life and death		
3 Marriage and the family		
4 Community cohesion		

Section 1

Section	One example of media storyline/ article about religion	One example of media storyline/ article about religion	How it may affect a person's attitude to belief in God
1 Believing in God			

Summary

- Many media programmes deal with issues of religion and community cohesion.
- These programmes are not always fair to religious beliefs.

examzone

Know Zone
Religion and community cohesion

Quick quiz

1 What is meant by 'discrimination'?

2 What is meant by 'ethnic harmony'?

3 How have attitudes towards gender roles in the UK changed in recent years?

4 Which Christian Churches do not allow women as religious leaders?

5 Give an example of how the government has tried to promote community cohesion.

6 What is a multi-faith society?

7 What is meant by 'community cohesion'?

8 Why do some Christians believe that Christianity is the only true religion?

9 What are the advantages and disadvantages of living in a multi-faith society?

10 Name and explain an example of how religion and community cohesion have been presented in a TV soap.

Plenary activity

Create two characters, one male and one female. Both are in their twenties. The man is a Muslim and the woman is a Christian. They have fallen in love and decide to get married in the UK. Using some or all of the material in this section, write a short report about the issues each of them face prior to their marriage and consider how these difficulties might be overcome.

Aim to get into the minds of these characters so they feel real to you and to someone who might read your report. Really try to get into the reasons why they believe and act as they do.

Find out more

A good way to find out more is to visit your local community centre, college or library and find out what multi-faith or multi-ethnic events are taking place in your area. For instance, there may be a carnival, or a local religious or ethnic group may be celebrating an important festival in the local park. Take the opportunity to pick up leaflets that will tell you what is going on and what it is all about. Remember to look in the local newspaper or listen to local radio and TV to find out what is going on in your local area.

Student tips

When I studied these topics for my GCSE, I made sure that I knew all the significant facts and understood all the main arguments for and against controversial issues. In this way, I could be sure of getting full marks for all the questions that asked for knowledge and understanding. For example, I could use my knowledge and understanding of the issues that cause racial tension to answer questions on the causes and possible solutions to such problems.

Self-evaluation checklist

Look at the following table. How would you rate your understanding of this topic? Use the following code to judge your status:

Green – I understand this fully.
Orange – I am confident I can answer most questions on this
Red – I need to do a lot more work on this topic.

Now answer the following questions:

- Do you hold an opinion on this topic and could you give reasons for that opinion if asked?
- Can you give the opinion of someone who disagrees with you and give reasons they hold this opinion?

Content covered	My understanding is red/orange/ green	Can I give my opinion?	Can I give an alternative opinion?
Government action to promote community cohesion.			
Changing attitudes to the roles of women.			
Christian attitudes to the equal role of women and the reasons for them.			
UK as a multi-ethnic society.			
Why Christians should promote racial harmony.			
The work of one Christian church with asylum seekers.			
UK as a multi-faith society.			
Different Christian attitudes to other religions and the reasons for them.			
Issues raised by a multi-faith society.			
Ways in which religions work to promote community cohesion.			
How an issue from this topic has been covered in the media and whether it was fair to religious people or beliefs?			

Know Zone
Religion and community cohesion

Introduction

In the exam you will see a choice of two questions on this section. Each question will include four tasks, which test your knowledge, understanding and evaluation of the material covered. A 2-mark question will ask you to define a term; a 4-mark question will ask your opinion on a point of view; an 8-mark question will ask you to explain a particular belief or idea; a 6-mark question will ask for your opinion on a point of view and ask you to consider an alternative point of view.

Give a glossary definition. You do not need to write any more – often this can be done in one sentence.

The 'explain why' questions are asking you to give reasons. In this case the best way would be to give four reasons and explain them fully. It is possible to get to the highest level with two reasons but you must develop them fully. Once the examiner has awarded the level for your answer, they will look at the quality of your spelling and punctuation and use this to decide if you gain 7 or 8 marks. Be aware on the C questions to use formal English and check your spellings etc.

Mini exam paper

(a) What is a **multi-ethnic society**? (2 marks)

(b) Do you think that women should have equal rights in religion?
Give **two** reasons for your point of view. (4 marks)

(c) Explain why mixed-faith marriages can cause problems for religious families. (8 marks)

(d) 'If everyone were religious there would be no racism.'
In your answer you should refer to at least one religion.

   (i) Do you agree? Give reasons for your opinion. (3 marks)

   (ii) Give reasons why some people may disagree with you. (3 marks)

Give your opinion. Note, however, that marks are only awarded for the reasons you have for thinking that opinion is correct. Each reason needs to be explained to gain the marks available.

The (d) question is split into two parts – answer each part separately. You must refer to the statement and Christian beliefs during this whole question. It may be worth considering whether Christians would agree or disagree with this statement and use their reasons in (ii) and then provide the alternative point of view as your own.

(i)   You must give one very well explained reason for your opinion or three simple reasons to gain full marks.

(ii)   You must now show that you understand the reasons that someone might disagree with you.

Mark scheme

(a) You will earn **2 marks** for a correct answer, and 1 mark for a partially correct answer.

(b) To earn up to the full **4 marks**, you need to give two reasons and to develop them fully. Two brief reasons will earn **2 marks** and one reason without development will earn **1 mark**.

(c) You can earn **7–8 marks** by giving up to four reasons, but the fewer reasons you give, the more you must develop them. You are being assessed on your use of language so you also need to take care to express your understanding in a clear style of English, and to make some use of specialist vocabulary.

(d) To go beyond **3 marks** for the whole of this question, you must refer to Christianity. The more you are able to develop your reasons, the more marks you will earn. Three simple reasons can earn you the same mark as one fully developed reason.

ResultsPlus

Maximise your marks

(c) Explain why mixed-faith marriages may cause problems for religious families. (8 marks)

Student answer	Examiner comments	Improved student answer
Mixed-faith marriages cause problems to religious families because the family may feel that their religion is right and the other religion is wrong.	The candidate has given a reason but this has not been developed fully. Develop this reason to explain why this is a problem.	Mixed-faith marriages may cause problems for religious families because members will have different beliefs and values. For example, the couple will need to agree on how to bring up their children, and what religion their children will belong to. There could be controversy over key issues such as homosexuality and arranged marriages.
Also, they may feel that if their son or daughter is getting married, that they will have to change their religious faith and join a religion whose teachings they do not believe in.	Again, a good reason is given but this is not developed. To gain top marks candidates need to say more about why mixed-faith marriage causes problems, not just what the problems are.	If one of the two people getting married decides to practise a different religion to suit their partner's family, this might cause worry and concern. For example, family members might worry that practising a religion that they haven't grown up with would be against the will of God, if the belief is not genuine.
Finally, the couple may not be able to have a religious wedding because of their different faiths and this means the family will not be able to celebrate the wedding properly.	This is another good reason which has not been developed. This answer will gain 4 marks, because the candidate has given some good reasons, but they have not really developed their answer. Using a good example can be very effective. In this case you could use an example as follows: if a Muslim and a Christian married and the children grew up as Muslims, the Christian grandparents may worry, for example, about whether or not the children could receive Christmas presents.	The couple may not be able to have a religious wedding because of their different faiths and this means the family will not be able to celebrate the union according to the traditions they believe in. Also, if a Muslim and Christian marry, for example, the Christian side of the family may worry about whether they should give Christmas gifts or not, and both sides could worry about how to deal with religious festivals.

Welcome to exam zone

Revising for your exams can be a daunting prospect. In this part of the book we'll take you through the best way of revising for your exams, step by step, to ensure you get the best results possible.

Zone In!

Have you ever become so absorbed in a task that suddenly it feels entirely natural and easy to perform? This is a feeling familiar to many athletes and performers. They work hard to recreate it in competition in order to do their very best. It's a feeling of being 'in the zone', and if you can achieve that same feeling in an examination, the chances are you'll perform brilliantly.

The good news is that you can get 'in the zone' by taking some simple steps in advance of the exam. Here are our top tips.

UNDERSTAND IT

Make sure you understand the exam process and what revision you need to do. This will give you confidence and also help you to get things into proportion. These pages are a good place to find some starting pointers for performing well in exams.

FRIENDS AND FAMILY

Make sure that your friends and family know when you want to revise. Even share your revision plan with them. Learn to control your times with them, so you don't get distracted. This means you can have better quality time with them when you aren't revising, because you aren't worrying about what you ought to be doing.

DEAL WITH DISTRACTIONS

Think about the issues in your life that may interfere with revision. Write them all down. Then think about how you can deal with each so they don't affect your revision.

COMPARTMENTALISE

You might not be able to deal with all the issues that can distract you. For example, you may be worried about a friend who is ill, or just be afraid of the exam. In this case, there is still a useful technique you can use. Put all of these worries into an imagined box in your mind at the start of your revision (or in the exam) and mentally lock it. Only open it again at the end of your revision session (or exam).

DIET AND EXERCISE

Make sure you eat sensibly and exercise as well! If your body is not in the right state, how can your mind be? A substantial breakfast will set you up for the day, and a light evening meal will keep your energy levels high.

BUILD CONFIDENCE

Use your revision time not only to revise content, but also to build your confidence in readiness for tackling the examination. For example, try tackling a short sequence of easy tasks in record time.

Planning Zone

The key to success in exams and revision often lies in good planning. Knowing **what** you need to do and **when** you need to do it is your best path to a stress-free experience. Here are some top tips in creating a great personal revision plan.

First of all, *know your strengths and weaknesses.*

Go through each topic making a list of how well you think you know the topic. Use your mock examination results and/or any other test results that are available as a check on your self-assessment. This will help you to plan your personal revision effectively, putting extra time into your weaker areas.

Next, *create your plan!*

Remember to make time for considering how topics interrelate.

For example, in PE you will be expected to know not just about the various muscles, but how these relate to various body types.

The specification quite clearly states when you are expected to be able to link one topic to another so plan this into your revision sessions.

You will be tested on this in the exam and you can gain valuable marks by showing your ability to do this.

Finally, *follow the plan!*

You can use the revision sections in the following pages to kick-start your revision.

109

MAY

SUNDAY	MONDAY	TUES
29	30	1

Be realistic about how much time you can devote to your revision, but also make sure you put in enough time. Give yourself regular breaks or different activities to give your life some variance. Revision need not be a prison sentence!

Find out your exam dates. Go to the Edexcel website **www.edexcel.com** to find all final exam dates, and check with your teacher.

Review Section
Complete t
Practice ex
question

Chunk your revision in each subject down into smaller sections. This will make it more manageable and less daunting.

Draw up a list of all the dates from the start of your revision right through to your exams.

13

Review Sectio
Complete three
practice exam

20

Review Sectio
Try the Keywor
Quiz again

Make sure you allow time for assessing your progress against your initial self-assessment. Measuring progress will allow you to see and be encouraged by your improvement. These little victories will build your confidence.

22

EXAM DAY!

27

28

29

Know Zone
Section 1: Believing in God

110

In this section, you need to show the examiner that you can understand the issues relating to belief in God (AO1) and that you can give your own point of view using reasons and evidence (AO2); you must also be able to give an alternative point of view and explain the reasons someone might think this.

The first step will be to learn the information. For this section it is things that cause people to believe in God and things that make people reject belief in God. You then must be able to explain how Christians respond to the arguments for not believing in God – in particular their

response to unanswered prayers, scientific explanations of the origins of the universe, and evil and suffering.

As part of the AO2 assessment you also have to be able to explain your own views, giving your reasons and evidence. You may find you agree with Christians or with the alternative arguments presented; you must be able to explain why. However, you must in the (d) questions be able to show that you understand that it is possible to have an alternative point of view from your own. You will be asked to give the reasons for this point of view.

Revision

Look back at the KnowZone at the end of the section on page 24. Complete the Self-evaluation checklist and think about areas you are stronger or weaker in, so that you can focus on those areas you are less confident about. You might like to try the Quick quiz or the Plenary activity at the end of the section, or the Support activity below. When you are ready for some exam practice, read through the KnowZone on pages 26–27. Then you could attempt the questions below.

Support activity

You will need to revise examples of two programmes about religions, in case a question on the media comes up in this section. As part of your revision, watch the programmes again. Jot down some notes either while you are watching or just after. You may like to consider these quotes and whether the programme supports or does not support the views:

- 'Religious programmes on television are usually supportive of religious believers.'

- 'Religious programmes on television say more about reasons not to believe in God than to believe in him.'

- 'Television programmes about religious beliefs discourage people from believing in God.'

Practice exam questions

(a) What is meant by **numinous**?
    (2 marks)

(b) Do you think God is the cause of the universe?
    Give **two** reasons for your point of view.
    (4 marks)

(c) Explain how Christians respond to the problem of evil and suffering. (8 marks)

(d) 'A religious upbringing brainwashes people into believing in God.' In your answer you should refer to Christianity.

    (i) Do you agree? Give reasons for your opinion. (3 marks)

    (ii) Give reasons why some people may disagree with you. (3 marks)

The material in this section tends to deal a lot more with issues that are not just of concern to Christians, but to everyone. We all care about matters of life and death because we will all die but, until we do, we want to be sure that our life and the lives of others, whether they are close to us or not, are treated with respect.

It is important in this section that you ensure you gain marks from considering the particular concerns of Christians – concerns that might be quite different from your own but that may also be shared by some non-religious believers.

Make sure you understand what it is that makes these views distinctive for Christians – issues such as the sanctity of life and the belief that God created human beings for a special purpose. For example, a Christian may say this is the reason they are against euthanasia; however a non-religious person may also be against euthanasia, because they think it is more important to preserve life than to take it away.

In this section it is also important to identify and understand why Christians have different attitudes to these issues.

Revision

Look back at the KnowZone at the end of the section on page 52. Read through the Self-evaluation chart and think about which your stronger and weaker areas are, so that you can focus on those areas you are less confident about. You might like to try the Quick Quiz or the Plenary activity at the end of the section, or the Support activity below. When you are ready for some exam practice, read through the KnowZone on pages 54–55. Then you could attempt the questions below.

Support activity

Question (d), about the paranormal is probably one of the trickier questions you could get, as it really is a matter of opinion, since no one can actually *prove* whether paranormal activity is genuine or not.

Your understanding of this area would be helped by finding out, as a class or in small groups, about some popular views on the paranormal. Find out about TV shows and so called 'celebrity' mediums, for example Tony Stockwell. They have an enormous following. Discuss why you think this is the case, and if there is anything that proves they are genuinely in touch with the paranormal.

Practice exam questions

(a) What is **resurrection**? (2 marks)

(b) Do you agree with abortion?

Give **two** reasons for your point of view. (4 marks)

(c) Explain why most Christians are against euthanasia. (8 marks)

(d) 'The paranormal proves that there is life after death.' In your answer you should refer to Christianity.

(i) Do you agree? Give reasons for your opinion. (3 marks)

(ii) Give reasons why some people may disagree with you. (3 marks)

Know Zone
Section 3: Marriage and the family

In this section you are presented with issues to which different groups of Christians have different attitudes. It is important to learn and understand where these different attitudes come from and to appreciate that not all Christians believe the same thing. In this section you will also have to address some more controversial issues that you have not thought of before. Take your time to think about your attitude towards them and why you hold that. It is also acceptable to say you do not know what you think yet, as long as you have considered all the different points of view.

Revision

Look back at the KnowZone at the end of the section on page 76. Read through the self-evaluation chart and think about which are your stronger and weaker areas, so that you can focus on those areas you are less confident about. You might like to try the Quick Quiz or the Plenary activity at the end of the section, or the Support activity below. When you are ready for some exam practice, read through the KnowZone on pages 78–79. Then you could attempt the exam practice questions.

Support activity

Question (b) on contraception (opposite) asks for your opinion without specifying that you refer to religion. It is a question that need not have anything to do with religion, but at the same time you need to make sure you show that you do understand religious views and that they might be held for special reasons. As a group or in pairs compare the attitudes towards contraception from the different Christian groups.

What do you think about the questions now, 'When does life begin?' and 'Is it ever right to kill?'. How might these questions be used in an argument about contraception? Do you agree with the use of contraception? Give reasons for your answer.

Practice exam questions

(a) What is **re-marriage**? (2 marks)

(b) Do you think it is right to use contraception?

Give **two** reasons for your point of view. (4 marks)

(c) Explain why some Christians allow divorce and some do not. (8 marks)

(d) 'Family life is more important for religious people than for non-religious people.' In your answer you should refer to Christianity.

   (i) Do you agree? Give reasons for your opinion. (3 marks)

   (ii) Give reasons why some people may disagree with you. (3 marks)

Rather like Matters of life and death, the issues you study in the section on Religion and community cohesion are ones of public concern, not just of concern to Christians. Your task in the exam is to show that you understand how Christians tackle these issues, and also that you understand the beliefs underlying their attitudes to matters of community cohesion.

These issues are important for society as well as for religion, but you need to distinguish between these in the exam. For example, a question asking if you agree there should be equal rights for women in religion demands a different response from you than if the question asked whether women should have equal rights in society.

Revision

Look back at the KnowZone at the end of the section on page 104. Read through the Self-evaluation chart and think about which your stronger and weaker areas are, so that you can focus on those areas you are less confident about. You might like to try the Quick Quiz or the Plenary activity at the end of the section, or the Support activity below. When you are ready for some exam practice, read through the KnowZone on pages 106–107. Then you could attempt the questions below.

Exam question tips for **all sections**

Questions of type (a)

Your answers should give the glossary definitions of the key words! Make sure you know them!

Questions of type (b)

These questions are seeking your opinion, BUT you will only get marks if you go beyond describing what you think. Your answer must be supported by TWO reasons and you need to explain how these reasons support your opinion.

Questions of type (c)

Questions here are asking you either:
to explain *why*…, which demands the word *because*….

or:

to say how two things are connected, e.g the examiner is looking for evidence that you understand how the religious teachings or beliefs affect the actions of believers. It is an explanation of the how the two things are connected *not* a description of them.

Questions of type (d)

Answers must be a response to the statement, so make sure that this is what you do.

Give your reasons for agreeing or not agreeing with the statement. If you agree with the Christian response, then say so, and then give the alternative point of view in part (ii). Or use the Christian response for the alternative viewpoint.

If you are not sure – make it up! No one is going to check that you still hold these views, but they must be supported by reasons

Practice exam questions

(a) What is **racism**? (2 marks)

(b) Do people from a different religion have the right to try to convert you?

Give **two** reasons for your point of view. (4 marks)

(c) Explain why Christians should help to promote racial harmony. (8 marks)

(d) 'Women should have the same rights as men in religion.' In your answer you should refer to Christianity.

(i) Do you agree? Give reasons for your opinion. (3 marks)

(ii) Give reasons why some people may disagree with you. (3 marks)

As you get close to completing your revision, the Big Day will be getting nearer and nearer. Many students find this the most stressful time and tend to go into panic mode, either working long hours without really giving their brains a chance to absorb information, or giving up and staring blankly at the wall.

Panicking simply makes your brain seize up and you find that information and thoughts simply cannot flow naturally. You become distracted and anxious, and things seem worse than they are. Many students build the exams up into more than they are. Remember: the exams are not trying to catch you out. If you have studied the course, there will be no surprises on the exam paper!

Student tip

I know how silly it is to panic, especially if you've done the work and know your stuff. I was asked by a teacher to produce a report on a project I'd done, and I panicked so much I spent the whole afternoon crying and worrying. I asked other people for help, but they were panicking too. In the end, I calmed down and looked at the task again. It turned out to be quite straightforward and, in the end, I got my report finished first and it was the best of them all!

In the exam you don't have much time, so you can't waste it by panicking. The best way to control panic is simply to do what you have to do. Think carefully for a few minutes, then start writing and as you do, the panic will drain away.

Don't panic

You will have one and a half hours for this exam paper and in that time you have to answer **four** questions, one on each of the four sections you have studied: Believing in God, Matters of life and death, Marriage and the family, Religion and community cohesion.

In each section, you can make a choice from two questions.

Each question will be made up of four different parts:

- a 2-mark question will ask you to define a term
- a 4-mark question will ask your opinion on a point of view
- an 8-mark question will ask you to explain a particular belief or idea
- a 6-mark question will ask for your opinion on a point of view and ask you to consider an alternative point of view.

Effectively you shouldn't spend more than 22.5 minutes on each section (that's 90 minutes divided by 4):

- the 8-mark question deserves the most attention, so that's around 9 minutes
- the 2-mark question should take you 1.5 minutes, then
- 5 minutes for the 4-mark question, and
- the remaining 7 minutes for the 6-mark question.

Obviously you can give or take here or there, and your teacher may guide you differently, but as long as you don't go over 22.5 minutes altogether and the length of each of your answers is appropriate for the number of marks available, then you'll be on the right lines.

Meet the exam paper

This diagram shows the front cover of the exam paper. These instructions, information and advice will always appear on the front of the paper. It is worth reading it carefully now. Check you understand it. Now is a good opportunity to ask your teacher about anything you are not sure of here.

Print your surname here, and your other names afterwards. This is an additional safeguard to ensure that the exam board awards the marks to the right candicate.

Here you fill in the school's exam number.

Ensure that you understand exactly how long the examination will last, and plan your time accordingly.

Note that the quality of your written communication will also be marked. Take particular care to present your thoughts and work at the highest standard you can, for maximum marks.

Here you fill in your personal exam number. Take care when writing it down because the number is important to the exam board when writing your score.

In this box, the examiner will write the total marks you have achieved in the exam paper.

Make sure that you understand exactly which questions from which sections you should attempt.

Don't feel that you have to fill the answer space provided. Everybody's handwriting varies, so a long answer from you may take up as much space a short answer from someone else.

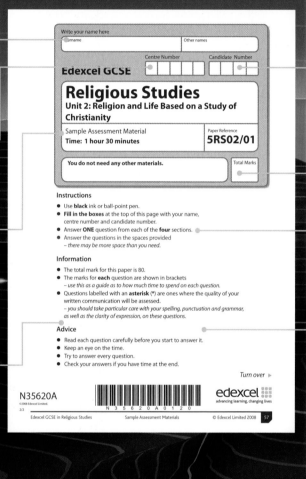

Practical tips on the exam paper

- You must use a black pen. Your paper is scanned into a computer for marking. If you write in any other colour, you risk your work not being seen clearly.

- You must choose your question carefully – cross out the one you are not going to do – to avoid changing a question half-way through answering it. This is a very common mistake and costs candidates lots of marks!

- Mark with an x at the top of the page which question you have chosen.

- Do not write outside the guidelines – your answer may get cut off by the scanning process.

- Do not use extra sheets and attach them unless it is absolutely necessary. If you need more space – for example, for a (b) question – continue into the (c) space and when you change question write your own (c). Do the same for (c) into (d). If you then run out, put an arrow and write at the end of the exam booklet.

Zone Out

This section provides answers to the most common questions students have about what happens after they complete their exams. For more information, visit the ExamZone website. Go to www.heinemann.co.uk/hotlinks (express code 4202P) and click on the appropriate link.

About your grades

Whether you've done better than, worse than, or just as you expected, your grades are the final measure of your performance on your course and in the exams. On this page we explain some of the information that appears on your results slip and tell you what to do if you think something is wrong. We answer the most popular questions about grades and look at some of the options facing you.

When will my results be published?

Results for summer examinations are issued on the **middle** two Thursdays in August, with GCE first and GCSE second. November exam results are issued in January, January exam results are issued in March and March exam results are issued in April.

Can I get my results online?

Visit the resultsplus direct website. Go to www.heinemann.co.uk/hotlinks (express code 4202P) and click on the appropriate link, where you will find detailed student results information including the 'Edexcel Gradeometer' which demonstrates how close you were to the nearest grade boundary.

I haven't done as well as I expected. What can I do now?

First of all, talk to your subject teacher. After all the teaching that you have had, tests and internal examinations, he/she is the person who best knows what grade you are capable of achieving. Take your results slip to your subject teacher and go through the information on it in detail. If you both think there is something wrong with the result, the school or college can apply to see your completed examination paper and then, if necessary, ask for a re-mark immediately. The original mark can be confirmed or lowered, as well as raised, as a result of a re-mark.

How do my grades compare with those of everybody else who sat this exam?

You can compare your results with those of others in the UK who have completed the same examination using the information on the Edexcel website. Go to www.heinemann.co.uk/hotlinks (express code 4202P) and click on the appropriate link.

I achieved a higher mark for the same unit last time. Can I use that result?

Yes. The higher score is the one that goes towards your overall grade. Even if you sat a unit more than twice, the best result will be used automatically when the overall grade is calculated. You do not need to ask the exam board to take into account a previous result. This will be done automatically so you can be assured that all your best unit results have gone into calculating your overall grade.

What happens if I was ill over the period of my examinations?

If you become ill before or during the examination period you are eligible for special consideration. This also applies if you have been affected by an accident, bereavement or serious disturbance during an examination.

If my school has requested special consideration for me, is this shown on my Statement of Results?

If your school has requested special consideration for you, it is not shown on your results slip, but it will be shown on a subject mark report that is sent to your school or college. If you want to know whether special consideration was requested for you, you should ask your Examinations Officer.

Can I have a re-mark of my examination paper?

Yes, this is possible, but remember that only your school or college can apply for a re-mark, not you or your parents/carers. First of all, you should consider carefully whether or not to ask your school or college to make a request for a re-mark. It is worth knowing that very few re-marks result in a change to a grade – not because Edexcel is embarrassed that a change of marks has been made, but simply because a re-mark request has shown that the original marking was accurate. Check the closing date for re-marking requests with your Examinations Officer.

When I asked for a re-mark of my paper, my subject grade went down. What can I do?

There is no guarantee that your grades will go up if your papers are re-marked. They can also go down or stay the same. After a re-mark, the only way to improve your grade is to take the examination again. Your school or college Examinations Officer can tell you when you can do that.

How many times can I re-sit a unit?

You may resit a modular GCSE Science or Mathematics module test once, prior to taking your terminal examination and before obtaining your final overall grade. The highest score obtained on either the first attempt or the re-sit counts towards your final grade. If you enter a module in GCSE Mathematics at a different tier, this does not count as a re-sit. If you are on the full modular Religious Studies GCSE course, and sat the first unit last year, you may re-sit module 1 when you sit module 2 to maximise your full course grade.

For much more information, visit the Examzone website. Go to www.heinemann. co.uk/hotlinks (express code 4202P) and click on the appropriate link.

Glossary

This is an extended glossary containing definitions that will help you in your studies. Edexcel key terms are not included as all of these are defined in the lessons themselves.

Analogy – A way of comparing two different things to highlight their similarities.

Annulment – A declaration by the Church that a marriage never lawfully existed.

Asylum seeker – Someone who formally requests permission to live in another country because they (and often their families) have a 'well-founded fear of persecution' in their country of origin.

Baptism – The Christian **initiation ceremony** that welcomes a person into the Christian community.

Bible – The sacred text of Christianity.

'Big bang' theory – The theory that an enormous explosion started the universe around 15 billion years ago.

Catechism – The official teachings of the **Roman Catholic** Church.

Causation – The belief that nothing happens by chance and that everything has a reason or a cause.

Church school – A school that educates children within a Christian environment.

Civil – When linked with marriage, this means without religious ceremony.

Cohesion – The action of forming a united whole.

Communion of the saints – The belief that Christians will live on after death and that living Christians can share with those who have died.

Conception – The moment when sperm and ovum meet in a woman's body to form an **embryo**.

Confirmation – The service (**sacrament**) when people confirm for themselves the promises made for them in infant baptism.

Corruption – When people in government act dishonestly in return for money or personal gain.

Counselling – Special help and advice given to people who have personal, social or other problems.

Déjà vu – The feeling of having already experienced the present situation; for example, when a place feels familiar, even though you are sure you have never been there before.

Design – The appearance of order and purpose.

Divorce – The legal termination of a marriage.

DNA – A substance present in nearly all living organisms that carries genetic information.

Embryo – An unborn baby up to eight weeks old, before it becomes a foetus.

Equality – The state of everyone having equal rights regardless of their gender, race or class.

Ethnic – Relating to a group of people having a common national or cultural tradition.

European Union – A group of European countries that have joined together for economic and trade reasons.

Evolution – The gradual development of species over millions of years.

Exclusivism – see **Religious exclusivism**

Extended family – Children, parents and grandparents/ aunts/uncles living as a unit or in close proximity.

Extra-marital sex – Sex that takes place outside, or before, **marriage**.

Faith – Belief in something without total proof.

Foetus – An unborn baby at least eight weeks old.

Fundamentalism – The belief that the Bible is fact; that it is true in every way.

Gender – The state of being male or female, especially in social or cultural contexts.

Harmony – Agreement between people, especially when they live together in peace.

Hospice – A type of hospital where the terminally ill are cared for and prepared for death.

Immigration – Coming to live permanently in a foreign country.

Inclusivism – see **Religious inclusivism**

Initiation ceremony – A ritual, such as **baptism**, that welcomes a person as a new member of a community or group that holds a certain set of beliefs.

Judgement – The act of judging people and their actions.

Justice – Correct allocation of reward and punishment; doing what is right and fair.

Legislation – The name for all the laws dealing with a particular topic, for example 'health legislation' or 'traffic legislation'.

Marriage – The condition of a man and woman being legally united for the purpose of living together and usually having children.

Medium – A person who claims to be able to communicate between the dead and the living.

Methodism – A branch of Christianity that came into existence through the work of John Wesley in the 18th century.

Migrant worker – A person who travels from place to place, especially to a different country, in search of work.

New Testament – The second part of the Bible, which records the life of Jesus and the early Church.

Parable – A simple story used to illustrate a moral or spiritual lesson.

Passive – Accepting or allowing what happens or what others do, without resistance.

Poverty – The state of being extremely poor.

Priest – Specially called or chosen person who is ordained to be a minister of the **sacraments**.

Protestant – That part of the Christian Church that became distinct from the **Roman Catholic** and other churches, when their members 'protested' the centrality of the **Bible** and other beliefs.

Programmes about religion – Programmes where religion is the main feature or way of presenting an idea or story.

Religious exclusivism – Belief that true Christians will go to heaven and others will be excluded.

Religious inclusivism – Belief that all religions lead to God but that Christianity is the only religion with the full truth.

Roman Catholic – That part of the Christian Church owing loyalty to the Pope in Rome.

Sacrament – An outward sign of something holy, usually representing an aspect of God's relationship with human beings.

Same-sex family – Two same-sex parents and their children.

Séance – A meeting at which people attempt to contact the dead.

Single-parent family – One parent living alone with their children as a result of divorce, separation or death, or because the parent is unmarried.

Stewardship – Looking after something so it can be passed on to the next generation.

Ten Commandments – The divine rules of conduct given by God to Moses and set out in the second book of the **Bible**.

Terminal illness – An illness with no cure from which a person will eventually die.

Tolerance – The willingness to accept different cultures and the practices of other religions, nationalities, etc.

Vision – An experience of seeing something in a dream or trance.

Worship – Praising God.

Index

In the following index, main entries of key terms are given in bold type and the page number that is also in bold will lead you to a definition of the word. For further definitions of unfamiliar words, see also the Glossary on pages 118–19.